D0203849

DATE DUE

EDWARD BURLINGAME HILL

Edward Burlingame Hill. Courtesy of George E. B. Hill

EDWARD BURLINGAME HILL

A Bio-Bibliography

LINDA L. TYLER

BIO-BIBLIOGRAPHIES IN MUSIC, NUMBER 21
Donald L. Hixon, Series Adviser

Greenwood Press
New York • Westport, Connecticut • London

Library of Congress Cataloging-in-Publication Data

Tyler, Linda L.
  Edward Burlingame Hill : a bio-bibliography / Linda L. Tyler.
    p.   cm. — (Bio-bibliographies in music, ISSN 0742-6968 ; no.
21)
  Discography: p.
  Includes index.
  ISBN 0-313-25525-3 (lib. bdg. : alk. paper)
  1. Hill, Edward Burlingame, 1872-1960—Bibliography. 2. Hill,
Edward Burlingame, 1872-1960—Discography. 3. Hill, Edward
Burlingame, 1872-1960. 4. Composers—United States—Biography.
I. Title. II. Series.
ML134.H46T9   1989
016.78′092′4—dc19   88-32343

British Library Cataloguing in Publication Data is available.

Library of Congress Catalog Card Number: 88-32343
ISBN: 0-313-25525-3
ISSN: 0742-6968

First published in 1989

Greenwood Press, Inc.
88 Post Road West, Westport, Connecticut 06881

Printed in the United States of America

The paper used in this book complies with the
Permanent Paper Standard issued by the National
Information Standards Organization (Z39.48-1984).

10 9 8 7 6 5 4 3 2 1

For Leigh

Contents

Preface

This volume charts the career of Edward Burlingame Hill,
American composer, educator, and writer. A music professor
at Harvard from 1908 until 1940, Hill helped train many
prominent American composers. Through his orchestration and
music history courses, his students learned about
orchestrating in the modern French manner and about the
latest European musical currents. Hill's own musical
compositions helped foster acceptance for turn-of-the-
century French innovations in the United States. Breaking
with the Teutonic tradition of his predecessors, he
integrated bold harmonic, instrumental, and textural
innovations into his music. Finally, as a writer, Hill
shared his openness to new musical styles with a wider
audience. He served as a Boston music critic for almost a
decade and also authored an important book and many journal
articles on contemporary music.

The first section of this study, a biographical and
interpretive essay, examines Hill's life and career within
the context of early twentieth-century American musical
culture. As a biographical inquiry, it is an attempt to
detail his multifaceted career as well as discern his
contributions to American music.

In the "Works and Performances" chapter, all of Hill's
musical compositions are listed, along with pertinent
information about them, such as date of composition,
instrumentation, dedication, premiere, and selected
performances. Each work is assigned an identifying number
preceded by "W" to facilitate cross-referencing between
chapters.

The next chapter, "Bibliography of Writings by Hill,"
offers an annotated list of the writings by Hill himself
(identifiers beginning with "H"). Then the "Bibliography of
Writings about Hill" annotates works that have been written

about him ("B"). Also listed in this chapter are reviews of
Hill's book and of his musical compositions.

The "Discography" chapter provides a list of all
commercially produced recordings of Hill's works, with each
item preceded by an identifier beginning with "D."

Appendices at the end of the work provide a list of the
archives housing sources pertaining to Hill and listings of
his works by alphabet, chronology, and opus number.

It is hoped that this work will serve as a useful guide
to other researchers, but will also stand on its own as a
needed study of an important musician who contributed much
to twentieth-century American music.

Acknowledgments

I would like to thank Professor Frederick K. Gable of the University of California, Riverside, who first encouraged and supervised my research into E. B. Hill's career. I am also grateful to friends and mentors at Princeton University, who stimulated further my interest in this topic.

I would also like to extend my appreciation to the librarians who assisted me in my work: Rodney G. Dennis and his staff at the Houghton Library, Harvard University; Sonia Moss of the Inter-Library Loan Department, Stanford University; Eleanor McGourty, archivist of the Boston Symphony Orchestra; and Nancy Johnson, Librarian of the American Academy and Institute of Arts and Letters.

Letters from and conversations with members of Hill's family--his son George Hill, daughters-in-law Esther Hill and Leelee Hill, and grandson Thomas Hill--provided valuable insights into the composer's life and career. Telephone conversations with Virgil Thomson and Jan LaRue, as well as a letter from Ross Lee Finney, also added to my understanding of Hill's work. For the sharing of their memories and ideas I am very grateful.

I would like to express appreciation both to Hill's family for permission to quote from his letters and music and to the Houghton Library for permission to cite from letters and manuscripts from its collection.

Finally, I would like to thank my husband, Leigh Eric Schmidt, for his encouragement and support. I dedicate this work to him with appreciation and affection.

EDWARD BURLINGAME HILL

Biography

In describing the music of Edward Burlingame Hill in 1942,
John Tasker Howard noted that

> If concert-goers expect a university professor to be
> academic in his own music, they are happily
> disappointed in Hill, for whatever they may possess,
> his works certainly lack a pedagogic flavor.[1]

In the early twentieth century, critics like Howard had come
to expect "academic" music from composers who taught in
colleges and universities. The first generation of music
professors--including John Knowles Paine and Horatio
Parker--had indeed proved conservative in their teaching
methods and musical tastes. They had guarded the hegemony
of German music: to be an "academic" composer at the turn
of the century implied the preservation of the Teutonic
order.

Edward Burlingame Hill, a professor at Harvard from 1908
until 1940, belied this expectation. In his teaching,
writings, and compositions, he exhibited an experimental
approach to music, one founded on the French <u>avant-garde</u>
rather than the German <u>status quo</u>. A supporter of French
music when "it was regarded as intensely radical," Hill
adopted the impressionist style into his own compositions as

---

[1] John Tasker Howard, <u>Our Contemporary Composers: American
Music in the Twentieth Century</u> (New York: Thomas Y.   Crowell,
1942), 57.

early as the 1910s.[2] Through his reviews as music critic in
the Boston Evening Transcript as well as his later book,
Modern French Music, and his articles, he forwarded this
appreciation of contemporary musical styles among American
audiences. Playing an important part in the musical
education of many Harvard-trained composers--including Roger
Sessions, Walter Piston, Virgil Thomson, Randall Thompson,
Ross Lee Finney, Elliott Carter, Irving Fine, and Leonard
Bernstein--Hill also exercised a formative influence on one
of the most innovative generations of American composers.
In short, through his multifaceted career as composer,
professor, and author, Hill did much to influence the
course of American music in the first half of the twentieth
century.

Edward Burlingame Hill was born on 9 September 1872 in
Cambridge, Massachusetts, the only child of Henry Barker
Hill and Ellen Grace (Shepard) Hill. Music was always
afforded a prominent place in the Hill home. Henry Hill
"sang the songs of Schubert and Franz, and was a great
admirer of Bach."[3] John Knowles Paine, Harvard's first
music professor, and William F. Apthorp, music critic of the
Boston Evening Transcript, counted among the elder Hills'
close friends and often participated in musical evenings at
the family's home.[4] E. B. Hill's later decision to pursue a
career in music no doubt had roots in this early exposure to
such music and musicians.

Hill entered Harvard College in 1890, having attended
Browne and Nichols School from 1884 until 1889. The
composer was a Harvard man born and bred. His grandfather
Thomas Hill had served as President of Harvard from 1862 to
1868. His father had become a member of the Chemistry

---

[2] Edward Burlingame Hill, quoted in David Ewen, ed.,
Composers of Today: A Comprehensive Biographical and
Critical Guide to Modern Composers of All Nations (New York:
H.W. Wilson, 1934), 112.

[3] Ibid.

[4] Ibid. and Walter Raymond Spalding, Music at Harvard:
A Historical Review of Men and Events (New York: Coward-
McCann, Inc., 1935), 202. Apthorp also dedicated his book
Musicians and Music-Lovers and Other Essays (New York:
Scribner's, 1894) to Henry Barker Hill. The composer owed
his first and middle names to another friend of his father.
While studying at the University of Berlin in 1869, Henry
Hill became classmate and friend of Edward L. Burlingame,
whose father, Anson Burlingame, served as the Chinese envoy
to the Court of Prussia. Charles Loring Jackson,
"Biographical Memoir of Henry Barker Hill, 1849-1903,"
National Academy of Sciences. Biographical Memoirs 5
(1905), 258.

faculty there in 1870. The composer went to Harvard, in his own words, "as a matter of course."[5]

At the time Hill matriculated, Harvard's music division, some two decades old, was a one-professor department. John Knowles Paine had become university organist and music director of the College in 1862. Offering to teach courses in harmony, counterpoint, and musical form, Paine was officially assigned two lecture courses in 1863--Musical Form and Instruction in Counterpoint and Fugue.[6] In the late 1860s and early 1870s, as curriculum policies underwent substantial changes--including the implementation of an elective system--music gained a greater foothold in the college offerings. When courses were first listed under departmental headings in 1871-72, the music division was formally recognized as a department--the first music department in the United States. Paine was named a full professor four years later, in 1875, and taught alone in the department until 1895, when Walter Spalding joined the faculty.

Between 1890 and 1894, when Hill attended Harvard, Paine's teaching repertory consisted in six courses, four of which he offered in any given year. These included classes in harmony, counterpoint, history of music, canon and fugue, free thematic music, and instrumentation. Hill graduated summa cum laude with an A.B. in music. His senior thesis, entitled "Program Music," traces the rise of descriptive music from the bird imitations in sixteenth-century songs to Richard Strauss's symphonic poems.[7] Hill concludes his work on a cautionary note: "Unless the program music possess a gist of appreciation of part writing, solidity of harmony and sense of form, its color and subtleties of depiction will go for naught."[8] Musical description, for Hill, forfeited much of its appeal if musical coherency were lacking.

Upon graduating, Hill evidently did not consider his musical training at Harvard sufficient. "I went to Harvard . . . and should do it again," Hill later commented, "altho it was impossible for me to get thoro technical preparation in college, Paine being an indifferent teacher."[9] Daniel Gregory Mason, a fellow Harvard student, corroborated this impression. "Hill and I have often compared notes on how much more rapidly we might have progressed in our purely

[5] Hill, quoted in Ewen, Composers of Today, 112.

[6] Spalding, Music at Harvard, 161.

[7] This thesis appears in installments in Music 20 (1901), 26-31, 76-84, 161-166, 225-229, 391-395.

[8] Ibid., 395.

[9] Hill, quoted in Ewen, Composers of Today, 112.

technical musical skill had we gone to a good conservatory instead of to Harvard."[10]

While perhaps not receiving a "thoro technical preparation" at Harvard, Hill did find ample opportunity to compose there. His earliest surviving composition, a one-movement Pastorale for String Quartet, is dated 1892. During his senior year, Hill completed a number of more ambitious works. He collaborated with Mason in composing the Hasty Pudding musical Granada (1894). He experimented in the song idiom with the "River Song" (1894).[11] And, most notably, he composed a four-movement Piano Sonata in F# minor (1894) for his summa cum laude award. He dedicated the sonata to Mason, "in appreciation of his advice and sympathy."[12]

During the four years following graduation, Hill continued his music study under a number of different teachers. In 1894-95, he studied piano and composition in Boston with B. J. Lang and Frederick Field Bullard. Lang had been a piano pupil of Alfred Jaëll and Liszt. He had also visited Wagner in Bayreuth in 1871 and was an honored guest at the premiere of the Ring in 1876. Bullard had studied composition with Josef Rheinberger in Munich from 1888 until 1892 and subsequently returned to Boston to teach harmony and counterpoint. Bullard also composed and published a number of songs.

During the next two years, 1895-97, Hill lived in New York City and worked under the tutelage of Arthur Whiting and Howard Parkhurst. Whiting had studied at the New England Conservatory and with Rheinberger in Munich and had taught harmony, counterpoint, and piano in Boston from 1885 until 1895. He moved to New York City in the same year as Hill, 1895. Parkhurst worked primarily as an organist in New York City but was also a composer of choral works.

Surviving compositions from this second student period, 1894-98, remain sparse. Hill completed one piano set--five Sketches after Stephen Crane (1895)--and at least two songs--"Danser la Gigue" (1896) and "All's Well" (1897). A letter to Mason from the summer of 1894 indicates that a compositional crisis of sorts may have temporarily impeded Hill's compositional efforts after graduating from Harvard.

> I have . . . been undergoing a radical musical
> reformation. I feel like some strange, abnormal fish

---

[10] Daniel Gregory Mason, "At Harvard in the Nineties," New England Quarterly 9 (1936), 70.

[11] A number of undated songs in an early hand also survive, but cannot be definitively attributed to his student days.

[12] Ink holograph of Piano Sonata in F# minor, Houghton Library, Harvard University.

> who can neither swim in water, nor live in earthly
> atmosphere. To plunge boldly into classicism seems a
> deliberate abandoning of originality, while
> picturesque is at present distasteful! In
> consequence I have written nothing, as everything I
> tried to start seemed equally blasphemous.[13]

This painful, youthful--if melodramatic--questioning of the
musical tastes and methods he had been taught at Harvard
offers perhaps an early indication of the broad-minded,
searching attitude he would later bring to his role as
composer and professor there.

The summer of 1898 proved pivotal for E. B. Hill's
compositional studies--indeed for his entire career. During
these months Hill lived in Paris and took composition
lessons from Charles Marie Widor and piano lessons from
Ludwig Breitner. Hill counted among the first American
composers to venture to France rather than to Germany for
his compositional training. Most composers of the
generation preceding his--Paine, Horatio Parker, George
Chadwick, Edgar Stillman Kelley, and Arthur Whiting, for
example--chose to study composition with German teachers.
Even the majority of Hill's contemporaries still opted for
Teutonic training. Frederick Shepherd Converse and Louis
Adolphe Coerne studied with Josef Rheinberger in Munich;
Henry Kimball Hadley worked with Mandyczewski in Vienna;
Rubin Goldmark with Robert Fuchs in Vienna; and Charles
Sanford Skilton at the Berlin Hochschule für Musik.

Exceptions to this rule, however, bear mention--and
perhaps provide clues to Hill's decision to go to Paris in
1898. Edward MacDowell had studied piano in Paris for three
years (1876-79) before opting to take up composition lessons
in Germany. While a student at Harvard, Hill had admired
MacDowell's music very much. "In those college days," as
Mason put it, Hill fell "much under the spell of
MacDowell."[14] While Hill never specifically cited the older
composer's study in Paris as an influence on his own
decision, the fact that one of the composers he admired most
had worked there may have increased the lure of the Parisian
option.

Another partisan of French music from Hill's student
years in Boston was Charles Martin Loeffler. Born in Alsace
in 1861, Loeffler emigrated to the United States in 1881 and
soon settled in Boston, becoming second chair in the first
violin section of the Boston Symphony Orchestra. His
compositions soon gained hearings by the orchestra: it
performed, for example, his Les veillées de l'Ukraine in
1891, Divertimento in 1895, and La mort de Tintagiles in
1898. In a later article he wrote on Loeffler, Hill claimed
that "Loeffler was from the first a figure of distinction in

---

[13] Quoted in Mason, "Harvard in the Nineties," 60-61.

[14] Mason, "Harvard in the Nineties," 59.

the musical life of Boston."[15] Loeffler's prominence in
Boston in the 1880s and 90s and the French orientation of
his compositions could well have provided added impetus to
Hill's decision to study in Paris.

Other musicians may also have influenced Hill's decision
to go to Paris. Hugo Leichtentritt, a classmate of Hill at
Harvard, had also pursued the Parisian option. Graduating
from Harvard in 1894, he went to Paris in 1894-95.
Similarly, Arthur Whiting, Hill's piano teacher in New York
in 1895-97, admired the music of Debussy, Ravel, and
Loeffler.[16] Arthur Farwell, perhaps an acquaintance of Hill
in Boston, also studied in France in the late 1890s.

Hill provides few details about his Parisian studies in
later autobiographical writings, but, given his later views
and compositional techniques, it would appear that he
steeped himself in the dynamic musical culture he found in
France. His teacher, Widor, professor of composition at the
Paris Conservatoire, could have provided access to prominent
composers--d'Indy, Saint-Saëns, Debussy, and Fauré--and was
well versed in the latest musical experiments. The concert
pianist Breitner, Hill's piano teacher in Paris, may also
have introduced Hill to contemporary French piano music and
perhaps to French musicians as well.

On returning to Boston in the fall of 1898, Hill began
teaching piano and harmony privately. During his seven
years of private teaching (1898-1905), he also composed
songs and short piano pieces. One of these piano pieces, <u>At
the Grave of a Hero</u>, was published by the Wa-Wan Press in
1903.[17] Hill also published two sets of piano pieces and a
set of songs during this period. Most of this music tends
toward a MacDowellian aesthetic and style, with song texts
and programmatic titles inspired by his New England
background. But novel harmonic experimentation--
especially with seventh and ninth chords--reveals inklings
of the new French persuasion. Example 1, from "Moonlight,"
the first of <u>Three Poetical Sketches</u> (1899), demonstrates
this early programmatic style.

On 12 June 1900 Hill married Alison Bixby.[18] Exactly one
year later their first son, Thomas Dana Hill, was born.

---

[15] Edward Burlingame Hill, "Charles Martin Loeffler,"
<u>Modern Music</u> 13 (1935-36), 27.

[16] Daniel Gregory Mason, <u>Music in My Time and Other
Reminiscences</u> (New York: The MacMillan Co., 1938), 78.

[17] This is available in the Wa-Wan reprint edition (New
York: Arno Press and the New York Times, 1970), 2:51-53.

[18] Alison Bixby Hill was noted to be "an antiquarian, a
charter member of the Chilton Club and a former president of
the Massachusetts Society of the Colonial Dames of America."
"Obituary," <u>New York Times</u> 3 March 1942, p. 23.

Example 1: "Moonlight"

Their second son, Henry Bixby Hill, arrived on 8 September 1905; and their third, George Edward Bellows Hill, on 24 April 1907.[19]

In 1902 Hill enrolled in a course in orchestration with George Chadwick at the New England Conservatory. This course, as Hill later wrote, "started me towards the orchestra, which has become one of my chief interests."[20] Indeed, Hill's orchestration techniques would prove the compositional element that critics would praise most highly later in his career. The orchestral work that Hill considered his most important early venture was <u>Jack Frost in Mid-Summer, Pantomime for Orchestra</u> (1908).

> My "chance" came when I was asked for a pantomime-ballet by the Boston (now New York) artist, Joseph Lindon Smith, for a benefit performance in aid of the Chicago Orchestra in 1908. I had the valuable experience of having this somewhat tentative music carefully rehearsed by Frederick Stock, and learned much as to orchestral effect.[21]

After this encouragement, Hill turned to the orchestra for a good portion of his subsequent works. Symphonic pieces became the best known and most widely performed pieces within his oeuvre. His later orchestration courses at Harvard also evoked high praise from many of his former students.[22]

In addition to studying orchestration, teaching privately, and composing during the first decade of the twentieth century, Hill also began writing about music. In November 1901 he became assistant music critic of the <u>Boston Evening Transcript</u>, a position he would hold off and on until 1908. During 1902-03 he also served as editor of the <u>Musical World</u>. He was a regular contributor to the journals <u>Etude</u> and <u>Musician</u> during the first decade of the twentieth century as well, writing articles aimed at piano teachers and piano students. These eight years as music journalist brought him into contact with a great deal of music and a great many musicians. He would continue to use his writing talents during his professorial career, contributing many articles to a variety of music journals.

---

[19] A fourth son, Edward Burlingame Hill, Jr., died at birth on 15 September 1912.

[20] Hill, quoted in Ewen, <u>Composers of Today</u>, 112.

[21] Ibid.

[22] See, for example, Virgil Thomson, <u>Virgil Thomson</u> (New York: Alfred A. Knopf, 1967), 61, and George Henry Lovett Smith, "Edward Burlingame Hill," <u>Modern Music</u> 16 (1939), 13.

In 1908 the Music Department of Harvard University offered Hill a one-year position to fill in for Walter Spalding. This began for Hill a thirty-two-year teaching career there. He remained an instructor for ten years. In 1918 he was promoted to assistant professor; in 1926 to associate; and in 1928 to full. He was chairman of the department from 1928 until 1935 and was named the James Edward Ditson Professor of Music in 1937. He retired in 1940. Hill spent most summers between 1908 and 1940 either in Europe or working on his musical compositions in Francestown, New Hampshire, where he had a "small workshop."[23]

Hill's teaching activities at Harvard encompassed a full range of assignments. The course that perhaps most influenced early Harvard-trained composers was Music 6, "Orchestration." Hill devoted a good part of the course to introducing each instrument to the class in a careful and systematic manner. To illustrate the various ways in which composers could write for each instrument, he pointed out important passages in symphonic works, most of which were drawn from the modern French repertory. He also invited members of the Boston Symphony Orchestra to demonstrate the possibilities and limitations of each instrument and allowed his students to write passages for the guests to play. After exposing his pupils to each instrument, Hill then had them orchestrate short piano pieces, again often drawn from contemporary French music. Through these lectures and exercises Hill honed his students' techniques in orchestrating in the turn-of-the-century French manner.

Another course which proved critical to the careers of many young American composers was Hill's class on modern French music. Hill designed the course himself and offered it for the first time in 1910-11. He called it "D'Indy, Fauré, Debussy: A Critical Study of Their Respective Contributions to Modern Music" (Music 4b). To help prepare for the course, Hill travelled the summer before to Paris, where he met Ravel, Debussy, and other French composers. This fully up-to-date course on French music proved of pivotal importance for many music students working at Harvard in the 1920s. Virgil Thomson noted, for example,

> Partly through [A. T.] Davison, himself French-trained, but even more through the views and musical ways of E. B. Hill, which were French to the core, I came in my Harvard years to identify with France virtually all of music's recent glorious past, most of its acceptable present, and a large part of its future.[24]

By familiarizing his students with the latest musical developments in France, Hill heightened the growing

---

[23] Hill, quoted in Ewen, Composers of Today, 112.

[24] Thomson, Virgil Thomson, 51.

conviction among many young composers that they should complete their musical education not in Germany, as most of their predecessors had, but in Paris.

In 1924-25 Hill unveiled another new class: Music 4d, "The Russian Nationalists from Glinka to Stravinsky." He was assisted this first year by Virgil Thomson. Just as Hill had introduced Harvard students to modern French music when it was considered unexplored territory, he took on modern Russian music, even up to the controversial Stravinsky. By staying abreast of the avant-garde in other countries and recognizing the importance of exposing his students to it, Hill put together two music history courses that did much to transform the contemporary music in his own country.

The remaining course that Hill taught on a regular basis at Harvard was Music 3, "History of Music from the Time of Palestrina to the Present Day."[25] Designed for students who had little or no musical background, the course offered Hill a challenge different from his other classes. But he seems to have thrived on it. "Nothing has interested me more," Hill claimed, "than my 'cinch' or 'pipe' courses in the history of music, in which I try to interpret its figures and their literature in terms which can appeal to the average non-technical student."[26] Hill's efforts seem to have found strong approval from the Harvard student body: after 1925-26 the course had to be limited to the first 100 students who signed up.

Advanced work in composition and orchestration with undergraduates and graduate students sometimes rounded out Hill's teaching duties. In these private sessions Hill concentrated on the special concerns of individual students. Most of these students turned to Hill for his expertise in orchestration rather than composition. In a twist on his assignments in his regular orchestration course, he sometimes had students in advanced study reduce orchestral pieces into piano pieces.

The list of Hill's students who went on to become accomplished composers and music educators is impressive. Timothy Mather Spelman (A.B. 1913), Samuel Barlow (A.B. 1914), Roger Sessions (A.B. 1915), Randall Thompson (A.B. 1920, M.A. 1922), Virgil Thomson (A.B. 1923, Teaching Assistant 1924-25), Walter Piston (A.B. 1924), Ross Lee Finney (attended as a graduate student in 1928-29), Elliott Carter (A.B. 1930 in English, M.A. 1932 in Music), Arthur Berger (attended in 1935-36), Irving Fine (A.B. 1937, M.A. 1938), Leonard Bernstein (A.B. 1939), and Jan LaRue (S.B. 1940, Ph.D. 1952) all studied with Hill at Harvard.

---

[25] After 1913-14, "Palestrina" was replaced by "Bach."

[26] Hill, quoted in Ewen, Composers of Today, 113.

Most of the composers who studied with Hill followed up
their Harvard years with study in Paris--often at his
suggestion. As early as 1914 Hill told Roger Sessions
confidentially that "we are not in a position here to give
you what you need. I won't go into the reasons why."[27] He
advised Sessions to work with Ravel in Paris after
graduating. While the war prevented Sessions from following
Hill's advice, others certainly accepted his counsel.
Thomson, Piston, Carter, Berger, and Fine all studied in
Paris after earning their degrees, with Finney having
studied there before coming to Harvard. The orientation of
Hill's courses and the example of his own works led many to
believe that the logical outgrowth of their Harvard
education was musical study in Paris.

While teaching these students at Harvard, Hill continued
to compose his own works. Neither he nor the university,
however, considered his compositional activities integral to
his position as professor. Instead, Hill and Harvard
looked upon his composing more as an avocation--an
independent endeavor he practiced outside of university
duties. Indicative of how Hill kept his two worlds of
teaching and composing separate was the way in which he
divided his year: "My summers," he wrote in 1934, "spent
for the most part in Francestown, New Hampshire . . . are
occupied with composition (there is no time for composing
during the academic year)."[28]

Besides being an activity limited to the summers,
composing was, Hill once claimed, "after all, a form of
'vice,' one which I would not forswear, or 'swear off.'"[29]
Sometimes he even combined this compulsion to compose with
other "vices." "I returned to nicotine August 11th," he
wrote to Amy Lowell in 1920. "Within twenty-four hours and
almost _ever since_ musical ideas have been buzzing in my
head. I have composed no magnum opus but nine waltzes for
piano, which I shall orchestrate and make of them an
agreeable lollipop."[30] Hill whimsically testified to this
source of inspiration in the name he first gave to the
piece. The title _Nicotiana_ is crossed out at the top of the
autograph, with the new title, _Nine Waltzes_, written
underneath.[31] Like nicotine, composition was a vice Hill

---

[27] Quoted in Ronald L. Davis, _A History of Music in
American Life_, 3 vols. (Malabar, Fla.: Robert Krieger
Publishing Co., 1981), 3:193.

[28] Hill, quoted in Ewen, _Composers of Today_, 112.

[29] Ibid., 113.

[30] Letter to Amy Lowell of 5 September 1920 in Houghton
Library, Harvard University.

[31] Ink holograph in Houghton Library, Harvard
University.

indulged in each summer. Hardly a year went by without the composition of a major piece.[32]

The university's small number of performing ensembles, and their independence from the music department, promoted this separation between Hill-the-teacher and Hill-the-composer. The Glee Club and the university orchestra (the Pierian Sodality), for example, both began as student clubs and were not closely tied into the department until 1912 and 1929 respectively.[33] They drew mostly from the standard canon for their repertory, with neither group performing a work by Hill except once: the Glee Club joined forces with the Boston Symphony Orchestra and the Radcliffe Choral Society to perform Hill's Ode for Mixed Chorus and Orchestra at the fiftieth anniversary concert of the Boston Symphony Orchestra in 1930. Hill relied much more on musical groups not officially affiliated with Harvard--the Boston Symphony Orchestra, the New York Symphony Society, and the Boston String Quartet, for example--for performance of his works.

Hill himself rarely took part in performing activities at Harvard. Unlike most other early music professors--Paine the university organist, Davison and Parker the choral directors, Woodworth the orchestra conductor--Hill did not actively participate in a performance program. This again helped widen the gap between his teaching and compositional activities. Because he took no active part in a university ensemble, he had no institutional outlet for his compositions on campus.

Hill focused his compositional attention on symphonic and chamber music during his professorial years. He virtually abandoned song and solo piano composition, the genres upon which he had drawn most often in his younger years. In the 1910s and early 1920s, Hill leaned toward a programmatic aesthetic, in keeping with the current fashion in Germany, France, and the United States. In works such as The Parting of Lancelot and Guinevere (1915), Stevensoniana Suite (1918), The Fall of the House of Usher (1920), Stevensoniana Suite No. 2 (1923), and Lilacs (1927), Hill attempted to evoke the atmosphere and spirit of particular literary models.[34] These programmatic works found approval from

---

[32] The composer's son George E. B. Hill related to the author that nicotine often caused Hill ulcers, forcing him to give it up during the school year, but that he nonetheless returned to it in the summers.

[33] Spalding, Music at Harvard, 107, 131.

[34] See the "Works and Performances" chapter for specific literary models.

critics and audiences alike.[35] The New York Symphony
Society and the Boston Symphony Orchestra hosted the
premieres of most of these works, with other orchestras
picking up the most acclaimed ones for a performance or two.

Critics were quick to note Hill's familiarity with
contemporary European trends in these programmatic works.
One reviewer claimed that Hill's "whole idiom is Wagnerian"
in Jack Frost,[36] while another declared that Stevensoniana
was related to "the modern French impressionistic school."[37]
Hill composed, as a Boston critic put it, in a "modern and
even ultra-modern" vein.[38] His orchestration often elicited
special note. "Mr. Hill," Henry Levine asserted, "has
achieved a shimmering orchestral color of genteel delicacy
and aristocratic refinement, an incessant shimmer and glint
in an ingenious play of timbres."[39] Welcomed by audiences
and critics as an American composer fully in step with the
best of contemporary European musical trends, Hill enjoyed
considerable success with his early programmatic symphonic
pieces.

Lilacs, Poem for Orchestra (1926) serves well as a
representative piece of this genre. Hill based the work on
Amy Lowell's poem "Lilacs." "Long an admirer of Miss
Lowell's poetry," Hill wrote in his program notes, "it one
day struck me forcibly that 'Lilacs' was an excellent
'subject' for musical treatment by one of New England
ancestry. On reflection, I soon saw the impractibility of
attempting to follow the poem in detail, and the present
work is the result of impressions connected with portions of
the poem, chiefly the beginning and the end."[40]

The work, about nineteen minutes long, has a formal
design of A B A' with a thirty-five-measure introduction.
Each of the three sections begins pianissimo, builds up to a

---

[35] His Stevensoniana Suite counted among the twenty-
five American works most frequently performed by leading
orchestras in the United States from 1919 to 1926. Daniel
Gregory Mason, The Dilemma of American Music and Other
Essays (New York: The MacMillan Co., 1928), 73.

[36] W. L. Hubbard, "Seein' Things at Night--The Musical
View," Chicago Daily Tribune, 7 Jan. 1908, 3.

[37] "Symphony Plays Work Illustrating Stevenson Poems,"
New York Herald, 18 Feb. 1918, 2:7.

[38] H. T. P[arker]., "The Symphony Concert," Boston
Evening Transcript, 25 Mar. 1916, 2:10.

[39] Henry Levine, "Two Symphonies and Visiting Soloists
Make Notable Calendar for Boston," Musical America 35/19 (4
Mar. 1922), 43.

[40] Edward Burlingame Hill, Boston Symphony Orchestra
Program 31 March 1927 (1926-27 season), 1688.

Example 2:   Themes <u>A</u> and <u>B</u> from <u>Lilacs</u>

full orchestral <u>forte</u> or <u>fortissimo</u>, then returns to a
soft, muted plane. The main themes, <u>A</u> and <u>B</u>, which generate
the main sections, are shown in Example 2. The sweeping,
legato lyricism of Theme <u>A</u> contrasts with the faster,
syncopated tightness of Theme <u>B</u>.

Perhaps most notable in <u>Lilacs</u> and in other programmatic
works by Hill is the orchestration. In <u>Lilacs</u> Hill utilizes
a large orchestra, including celesta, harp, piano, bass
drum, cymbals, and triangle, in addition to the conventional
ensemble, to achieve his shimmering sound.[41] Continually
changing his combination of instruments and limiting the
occasions on which he draws on the full orchestra, Hill
achieves a kaleidoscopic variety of sound. At the beginning
of the <u>B</u> section, for example, the violins and violas carry
the melody while the oboe and clarinet provide
countermelodies, the low strings hold out the tonic chord,
and the harp offers arpeggios on the tonic chord in an even
lower register. The winds then state Theme <u>B</u>, supported by
horns, <u>divisi</u> violas and second violins, a countermelody in
the cello, and high treble chords in the piano (Example 3).
This juxtaposition of novel combinations provides a good
example of Hill's mastery of instrumentation.

Example 3 also displays some of Hill's harmonic
techniques. The open fifths in the low strings and harp at
the beginning of the example; the dissonant intervals
resulting from counterpoint among the strings at first and
later between the oboe and English horn; the parallel
fourths in the piano and winds on the last page of the
example; and the melodic chromaticism, including the opening
E-natural of Theme <u>B</u>, which forms a tritone with the tonic,
A-flat, all testify to the way Hill built a personal
harmonic style out of the experiments of turn-of-the-century
French composers.

During the early 1920s, Hill also tried his hand at
composing for solo instruments and orchestra. In his
<u>Scherzo for Two Pianos and Orchestra</u> (1923-24) he

---

[41] The complete orchestration is 3(picc).3(engh).
3(bscl).3(cbsn) 6.3.3.1 timp, perc(3), cel, hp. pf, str.

Example 3: Lilacs

Example 3 (cont.)

Example 3 (cont.)

demonstrated his openness to another new musical style:
jazz. Hill counted among the earliest supporters of jazz
among "serious" composers.[42] He lectured to the League of
Composers on "Jazz and the Music of Today" on 10 February
1924 and wrote the article "Jazz" for the Harvard
Graduates' Magazine in 1926.[43] He also tried his hand at a
Quasi Fox Trot for clarinet and piano in 1919 and Jazz
Studies for two pianos in 1922. Hill's incorporation of
jazz elements into his more public Scherzo--syncopated
rhythms, seventh chords, and ambiguity between the raised
and lowered sixth--in 1923 confirmed his support of the new
idiom (see Example 4, mm. 3-8 of the piece). In a letter to
Oswald Villard of 1925, Hill assessed the Scherzo's limited
potential for success. "I fear it shares the fate of all
mulattos," he lamented, "in that it is too rowdy for the
purists, and not positive enough for the 'jazz-fiends.'"[44]

The Scherzo for Two Pianos and Orchestra was the first of
Hill's works to be performed under the baton of Serge
Koussevitzky. The Russian conductor had arrived in the
United States in 1924 to become leader of the Boston
Symphony Orchestra. He and Hill almost immediately became
good friends. Committed to performing works by
contemporary American composers, Koussevitzky considered
Hill an exciting discovery. Hill's Scherzo was the first
new American composition performed by the conductor after
his arrival in Boston. Hill's works, Koussevitzky claimed,
"show the mature intelligence and understanding of a true
artist, one who has the best interests of music as an art
always before him in the molding of his ideas."[45] Eleven
other works by Hill would find their premieres under the
baton of Koussevitzky over the next two decades. In
addition, Hill's influence with the conductor helped bring
about Boston performances of works by Walter Piston and
other former students.[46]

In the late 1920s Hill began to abandon the programmatic
trappings that characterized his early works for orchestra.
"I find myself in sympathy with those of the younger
generation," Hill wrote in 1931, "who feel that music has

---

[42] Nicolas Slonimsky, in "Composers of New England,"
Modern Music 7/2 (Feb.-Mar. 1930), 26, notes that "Hill is
perhaps the only New Englander to intrude on the New York
field by composing 'serious jazz.'"

[43] Mary Herron Dupree, "'Jazz,' the Critics, and
American Art Music in the 1920s," American Music 4 (1986),
289. Edward Burlingame Hill, "Jazz," Harvard Graduates'
Magazine 34 (1925-26), 362-365.

[44] Edward Burlingame Hill, letter to Oswald Villard of
14 April 1925 in Houghton Library, Harvard University.

[45] Quoted in Smith, "Edward Burlingame Hill," 11.

[46] Davis, History of Music, 3:107.

Example 4:   <u>Scherzo for Two Pianos and Orchestra</u>

enough intrinsic problems of its own without adding those of
other arts."[47]   In 1927 he composed his first non-
programmatic work, <u>Symphony in B-flat</u>.   This was followed by
<u>Symphony No. 2</u> (1929-30), <u>Sinfonietta for Orchestra</u> (1932),
<u>Sinfonietta for String Orchestra</u> (1936), <u>Symphony No. 3</u>
(1936), <u>Concertino for String Orchestra</u> (1939), and others.
In these works Hill eschewed descriptive titles and extra-

_____

[47] Edward Burlingame Hill, program notes, Boston
Symphony Orchestra program, 27 February 1931.

musical associations. He often, but not always, pared down
his orchestra, writing two works for string orchestra alone.
Sonata-allegro, scherzo-trio, and rondo schemes accounted
for the formal shape of most movements. "I have kept to the
traditional forms," Hill typically deprecated, "thinking I
had not had sufficient experience to experiment."[48]

Hill continued his foray into concerto and chamber music
composition as well. The Concertino in One Movement for
Piano and Orchestra (1931) and Concerto for Violin and
Orchestra (1933-34) premiered with the Boston Symphony
Orchestra, with Jesús Mariá Sanromá and Ruth Posselt as
soloists, respectively. In the field of chamber music, his
Sextet for Flute, Oboe, Clarinet, Horn, Bassoon and Piano
(1934) received the widest exposure and acclaim.
Commissioned by Elizabeth Sprague Coolidge and premiering at
the Berkshire Music Festival in 1934, the work was also
performed at the Rochester Festival of American Music in
1944 and the Columbia Festival of Contemporary Music in
1950. In addition, it was the first of three works by Hill
to be released on LP.[49]

Examples from one of Hill's "neo-classic" works suffice
to illustrate the salient features of his later style. The
Concerto for Violin and Orchestra (composed in 1933-34,
revised in 1937) serves as a good representative piece in
this regard. About twenty-five minutes long, the concerto
consists in three movements, each in sonata-allegro form.
Hill works within the framework of tonality in the piece,
yet stretches its boundaries through unconventional chord
progressions, quick modulations, an array of seventh and
ninth chords, and melodic chromaticism (see Example 5, mm.
1-20 of movement 1). In the short orchestral introduction
and opening theme, Hill makes pronounced use of syncopation,
meter changes, and short rhythmic motives (Example 5).
Indeed, many allegro themes in his neo-classic works seem
rhythmically rather than melodically motivated. Along with
this rhythmic interest, however, Hill carefully shapes his
opening violin solo to reach a final climax on g''' in m.
20.

With a fine sense of balancing new thematic material with
development, Hill states the first theme again, this time
with melodic variation and in a new key, C major (see
Example 6, mm. 26-30). With this second statement he moves
to D major and to his second theme, a slower, dolce melody
(see Example 7, mm. 42-57). While the orchestra provides an
undulating chordal backdrop rich in chromatic interest, the
violin plays a long legato line, replete with half and whole
notes, which reaches its high point on b''' in m. 48. Thus
Hill ably juxtaposes two moods--one rhythmically, the other
melodically oriented--in the course of about sixty

---

48 Ibid.

49 The other two were Stevensoniana Suite and Prelude
for Orchestra. See the "Discography" chapter.

Example 5: <u>Concerto for Violin and Orchestra</u>

Example 5 (cont.)

Example 6: <u>Concerto for Violin and Orchestra</u>

Example 7: <u>Concerto for Violin and Orchestra</u>

Example 7 (cont.)

measures. The orchestration of this piece contributes
deftly to its expression, with winds and brass featured most
prominently in the tutti sections.

   These neo-classic works drew generally favorable
reactions from critics and audiences. Claims of "modernism"
and "ultra-modernism" decreased during this phase, as
younger composers ventured into serialism and other atonal
realms. But Hill's workmanship, taste, and sense of
proportion were consistently praised from review to review.
His scoring techniques continued to receive particular
accolades. Leonard Bernstein, for example, wrote that
Hill's Symphony No. 3 "could easily supplant Scheherezade as
a schoolroom model" for orchestration.[50] Some critics, in
praising Hill's works, noted that they sounded
"unprofessorial." Lawrence Gilman claimed that the
Symphony in B-flat was "hearteningly free of the academic

   [50] Leonard Bernstein, "Season of Premieres in Boston,"
Modern Music 15 (1937-38), 105.

touch,"[51] and George Henry Lovett Smith noted that the
Concertino for String Orchestra was "scholarly without being
cerebral."[52] While adjectives such as "nostalgic,"
"conservative," and "retrospective" cropped up in a few
later reviews, Hill's music could not easily be denied its
due. If not reflective of the latest European trends, as
they once had been, Hill's compositions certainly continued
to "betoken the hand of a master craftsman."[53]

Alongside his compositional endeavors, Hill continued his
writing activities while teaching at Harvard. In the 1910s
he published several articles on contemporary composers,
including Fauré, d'Indy, Mahler, and Frederick S. Converse,
as well as a few on general trends in French music.[54]
Though not exhaustive in biographical detail or musical
analysis, these articles counted among the first to be
written about composers whose names were not widely
recognized at that time. Like his earlier reviews, these
articles helped introduce new composers and compositions to
the American listening and performing public. In 1915-17
Hill served as associate editor of the fourteen-volume study
The Art of Music and contributed two sizeable chapters to
the volume on Modern Music: "The Followers of César Franck"
and "Debussy and the Ultra-Modernists."[55]

Hill's writings were generally aimed at the musical
layperson more than the musical expert. Since the market
for specialized publications in music was so small during

---

[51] Lawrence Gilman, "An American Symphony Introduced
Here by Koussevitzy at the Last Evening Concert of the
Boston Orchestra," New York Herald Tribune, 13 Apr. 1928, 16.

[52] George Henry Lovett Smith, "Boston Premieres,"
Modern Music 17 (1939-40), 254.

[53] Grace Mary Stutsman, "Boston Orchestra Plays New
Symphonies," Musical America 57/19 (10 Dec. 1937), 12.

[54] Edward Burlingame Hill, "Gabriel Fauré's Piano
Music," Musician 16 (1911), 511; Edward Burlingame Hill,
"Vincent d'Indy: An Estimate," Musical Quarterly 1 (1915),
246-259; Edward Burlingame Hill, "Gustave Mahler," Musician
16 (1911), 585; Edward Burlingame Hill, "Frederick S.
Converse," Musician 14 (1909), 164-165; Edward Burlingame
Hill, "The Rise of Modern French Music," Etude 32 (1914),
253-254; Edward Burlingame Hill, "Significant Phases of
Modern French Music," Etude 32 (1914), 489-490; Edward
Burlingame Hill, "Synopsis of Modern French Music," Musician
17 (1912), 593, 666, 712, 742-743, 784; 18 (1913), 134-135,
350-351, 422-423.

[55] The Art of Music: A Comprehensive Library of
Information for Music Lovers and Musicians, ed.-in-chief
Daniel Gregory Mason; assoc. eds. Edward Burlingame Hill,
Leland Hall, and Ernest Newman; man. ed. César Saerchinger,
14 vols. (New York: National Society of Music, 1915-1917).

the 1910s and 20s, Hill and most other writers on music
eschewed detailed analysis in favor of non-technical
description. In fact, the style of Hill's articles
resembles that of his earlier reviews as critic for the
Boston Evening Transcript. He combines descriptive
summaries of the salient features of compositions with
terse, incisive assessments of their musical value and
importance. For example, Hill writes in his article on
d'Indy that the composer's Sonata for violin and piano

> may fall somewhat short of the profundity of the
> Second Symphony, but it too holds its place after an
> interval of ten years as a reaffirmation of d'Indy's
> technical and expressive mastery. If the method and
> plan of the work are obviously those of a devoted
> pupil of Franck, the themes (there are three
> generative phrases), the style and sentiment are
> overwhelmingly personal. If . . . [d'Indy] makes too
> great intellectual demands upon the listener to
> attain a similar popularity, it none the less
> deserves to be considered one of the significant
> specimens of its class since that of his master.[56]

It is in some ways unfortunate that Hill's mastery of such a
large repertory and his keen musical insight are allowed to
show through in only a general way in his writings. But
before the establishment of a large enough pool of readers
informed in musicological and theoretical matters, Hill and
most other writers on music addressed themselves to a wider
public.

In the early 1920s Hill wrote several articles for the
Revue musicale about contemporary American music.[57] In
these contributions Hill describes for French readers the
development of American music from about 1870, which he
cites as the beginning of "notre vie artistique sérieuse."
He also reports on some important Boston premieres of new
American and French compositions. Thus Hill not only sought
to promote French music in America, but also American music
in France. Also in the early 1920s, Hill accepted several
prestigious lecture engagements. In January 1920 he gave a
series of Lowell Lectures in Boston on "The Growth of French
Music." In 1921 he lectured on French music at the
University of Strasbourg and at the Congrès d'Histoire et de
l'Art at Lyons.

---

[56] Hill, "Vincent d'Indy," 254.

[57] Edward Burlingame Hill, "La musique aux tats-Unis,"
Revue musicale 2/3 (1921), 267-268; Edward Burlingame Hill,
"La musique américaine contemporaine," Revue musicale 4/1
(1922), 68-72 and 4/2 (1922), 171-173; Edward Burlingame
Hill, "La musique à Boston," Revue musicale 4/4 (1923), 75-
76; Edward Burlingame Hill, "La musique à Boston," Revue
musicale 7/6 (1926), 78-79.

Hill's research and publishing activities culminated in
1924 with his book, Modern French Music, an historical and
critical study of French music from Chabrier to Les Six.[58]
In the Introduction he argues for the preeminence of modern
French music over the contemporary music of other nations.

> Since the Franco-Prussian War, and to a large extent
> on account of it, French music has made almost
> incredible advances in technical mastery,
> originality, subtlety of expression, and above all in
> embodying national characteristics. . . . French
> music, through its exploration of new fields of
> harmonic effect, stylistic adaptability, clarity and
> fineness of emotional discrimination, has exercised
> an influence upon the entire civilized musical
> world.[59]

Hill goes on in his 384-page study to illuminate the seeds
of this movement in the decline of opera in late-
nineteenth-century France and the ascendancy of instrumental
music, brought about largely through the National Society of
Music and composers such as Saint-Saëns, Lalo, and Franck.
Individual chapters are devoted to Chabrier, the
"unquestioned pioneer of the progressive type of French
music,"[60] Fauré, d'Indy, Debussy, and Ravel. Hill groups
other composers into chapters entitled "The Heritage of
Franck," "Reflections from Literature," "Some Modernist
Types," and "A Group of Iconoclasts."

One of the questions that guides Hill through his survey
of each composer's oeuvre in Modern French Music is that of
influence: how a composer's style "is evolved gradually
from recognizable sources of absorption."[61] In his chapter
on Debussy, for example, Hill is as much interested in what
the composer inherited from Massenet, Chabrier, Fauré,
Satie, Balakirev, Rimsky-Korsakov, Mussorgsky, Wagner, gypsy
music, and the Symbolist poets as he is in Debussy's
individual contribution. Certainly Hill points up the
creative genius exhibited in Debussy's works, but even this
he regards with a certain air of inevitability. "The
inheritance of the Renaissance," Hill waxed eloquent, "had
not passed to the French nation for nought. [Debussy]
reverted to its spirit, fell in line with the past ages, and
then had the discernment to recognize that impressionism
offered the perfect counterpart to his musical thought."[62]

---

[58] Edward Burlingame Hill, Modern French Music
(Cambridge, Mass.: Houghton Mifflin Co., 1924; reprint ed.,
New York: Da Capo Press, 1969).

[59] Ibid., 2.

[60] Ibid., 60.

[61] Ibid., 190.

[62] Ibid., 238.

This approach to Debussy and other composers evidently found favor with Hill's reading audiences. Reviewers generally agreed with his assessment of the progress of French music. They praised his originality, thoroughness, and avoidance of biased presentation. A product of many years of research, many hearings of French music, and several trips to Europe, the book was among the first to grapple with an important repertory of contemporary music in a systematic and critical way.

After the publication of Modern French Music in 1924, Hill's publishing activities tapered off. Serving on the Advisory Board of Modern Music from its inception in 1924 to its final issue of 1947, he registered his support for the younger generation of composers in the publishing realm. He also contributed an article and two reviews to the journal.[63] A few more articles in other journals--one on jazz, another on Ravel--rounded out his written corpus.[64]

Hill retired from Harvard in 1940 and subsequently divided his time between Francestown, New Hampshire, and Sarasota, Florida. His active retirement yielded many new compositions, some of which found public performance. His Music for English Horn and Orchestra (1943), for example, was performed by the Boston Symphony Orchestra in 1945. His Prelude for Orchestra (1952-53) was commissioned by the Koussevitzky Music Foundation and premiered at their tenth annual concert in 1953. He also remained active in the National Institute of Arts of Letters, to which he had been elected in 1916, and wrote letters in behalf of several young composers in connection with the Institute until at least 1957.[65] Hill died at the age of 87, on 9 July 1960.

Hill received many honors throughout his life for his academic and musical endeavors. Besides being elected to the National Institute, he was chosen to serve on the International Jury for Musical Composition at the Olympic Games in Paris in 1924. He served as judge for the Paderewski Prize competition in 1934. France named him a Chevalier of the Legion d'Honneur in 1936. The University

----

[63] Hill, "Charles Martin Loeffler;" Edward Burlingame Hill, "Copland's Jazz Concerto in Boston," Modern Music 4/4 (May-Jun. 1927), 35-37; Edward Burlingame Hill, Review of Claire Reis's Composers in America, Modern Music 15 (1937-38), 197-198.

[64] Hill, "Jazz," and Edward Burlingame Hill, "Maurice Ravel," Musical Quarterly 13 (1927), 130-146.

[65] The latest is a letter to Aaron Copland of 28 November 1957 in behalf of John La Montaine for an Institute grant, American Academy and Institute of Arts and Letters Library.

of New Hampshire conferred on him an honorary musical
doctorate in 1951.[66]

Hill's contribution to American music as a composer is
easily obscured by the innovation and experimentation of
the generation that succeeded his. Yet Hill played an
important role in building an essential bridge to span the
conservative nineteenth century in America with the radical
twentieth. The conservative label pinned on Hill as a
composer beginning in the 1930s only confirms the
sturdiness of that bridge: precisely because he had helped
make turn-of-the-century French innovations a part of the
musical status quo, his music sounded retrospective as
younger composers readily used it to cross over to other
experiments. Hill's break with the tradition of his
predecessors in the 1910s and 20s and the superior
craftsmanship he brought to his works deserve signal
recognition when assessing early twentieth-century American
music.

But Hill's contribution to American music did not stop
with his compositions. He also left an important stamp on
the role of music educator in the university. Hill was
among the first to reconcile the role of music professor
with an openness to musical experimentation. Unlike his
predecessors and conservatory teachers, Hill did not
safeguard Teutonic ideals or insist that his students
conform to them. In his writings and teaching, he
demonstrated support for almost all new musical experiments.
As he put it, he had "a liberal attitude towards Stravinsky,
Schönberg, and Hindemith"[67] and took "real pleasure in
discord, lack of melody, . . . and unfathomable complexity
generally."[68] He communicated this openness to his
students, many of whom went on to lead the avant-garde in
American music for the next half-century. In the whirl of
festivals, concerts, and recitals devoted to performing
twentieth-century American music, the compositions of Edward
Burlingame Hill have, with many other distinguished
compositions, been too often relegated to the heap of old
novelties. But his legacy as a composer, writer, and
educator nonetheless continues long after his "modern" and
"ultra-modern" works have fallen into neglect in a "post-
modern" world.

---

[66] In 1952 Hill gave his collection of scores to the
University of New Hampshire.

[67] Hill, quoted in Ewen, Composers of Today, 112.

[68] Edward Burlingame Hill (letter of 1908 to the Class
of '94 Secretary), quoted in Harvard College Class of 1894,
Fiftieth Anniversary Report, 1894-1944 (Norwood, Mass.:
Plimpton Press, 1944), 256.

Works and Performances

This chapter provides a list of the musical works composed
by Edward Burlingame Hill and the public performances of
these compositions. The works are grouped first by genre,
then by date of composition. Each work and performance is
denoted with an identifying label beginning with the letter
"W".   Citations are cross-referenced with appropriate
entries in the "Bibliography of Hill's Writings" ("H"),
"Bibliography of Writings about Hill" ("B"), and the
"Discography" ("D") chapters: for example, "See D60" refers
the reader to the "Discography" chapter, item 60.   The
instrumentation given for orchestral works follows the
customary sequence: flutes, oboes, clarinets, bassoons;
horns, trumpets, trombones, tubas; timpani; percussion;
other instruments; strings.

Since so few of Hill's compositions were published,
locations of the manuscripts have been provided. Most of
his works exist in manuscript in ten cartons (uncataloged)
in Houghton Library, Harvard University (MH-H).

Abbreviations:

DLC: Library of Congress, Washington, D.C.
MB: Boston Public Library, Boston, Mass.
MBCM.:   New England Conservatory, Spalding Library, Boston,
          Mass.
MH-H: Harvard University, Houghton Library, Cambridge,
          Mass.
NNAL: American Academy of Arts and Letters, New York,
          N.Y.
NRU-Mus: University of Rochester, Eastman School of Music,
          Sibley Music Library, Rochester, N.Y.
OCU: University of Cincinnati, Gorno Memorial Music
          Library, Cincinnati, Ohio.

Orchestral Works

W1.   Overture to "She Stoops to Conquer", op. 12, 1904-06.

       Ink holograph in MH-H.

W2.   Overture for Full Orchestra, 1910.

       Ink holograph in MH-H (note on holograph: "Composed
       by Music 7" [composition course at Harvard]).

W3.   Fairy Scenes, Suite for Orchestra, op. 20, 1913.
          1. "Once upon a Time"
          2. "The Princess Sleeps"
          3. "The Jester"
          4. "The Prince's Serenade"

       Pencil holograph of nos. 1-4, ink holograph of no. 4,
       and part set for no. 4 in MH-H.

W4.   The Parting of Lancelot and Guinevere, Symphonic Poem
          after Stephan Phillips, op. 22, 1915.

       Duration 8'.
       3(picc).3(engh).3(bscl).3(cbsn) 6.3.3.1 timp,
          perc(5), glock, hp, str.
       Ink holograph in MH-H.

       Premiere:
W4a.   31 December 1915 and 1 January 1916, St. Louis
          Symphony Orchestra, Max Zach, conductor. See B37.

       Other Selected Performance:
W4b.   24 and 25 March 1916, Boston Symphony Orchestra, Karl
          Muck, conductor. See H174, B38-B43.

W5.   Stevensoniana Suite, Four Pieces for Orchestra after
          Poems from R. L. Stevenson's "A Child's Garden of
          Verses", op. 24, Sept. 1916 - Jan. 1917.
          1. "March"
          2. "Lullaby, 'The Land of Nod'"
          3. "Scherzo"
          4. "The Unseen Playmate"

       Duration 15'.
       3(picc).2.2.2 4.3.3.1 timp, perc(2), hp, str.
       Ink holograph in MB.
       Pencil and ink holographs and three part sets in MH-H.
       See D1.

Premiere:
W5a. 17 February 1918, New York Symphony Society, Walter
     Damrosch, conductor. See B52, B56, B61.

Other Selected Performances:
W5b. 12 April 1918, New England Conservatory Orchestra,
     Wallace Goodrich, conductor. See B49, B59.
W5c. 27 June 1918, Cincinnati Symphony Orchestra, at a
     concert of the Ohio Music Teachers' Association,
     P. A. Tirindelli, conductor. See B60.
W5d. 28 and 29 March 1919, Boston Symphony Orchestra,
     Henri Rabaud, conductor. See B44, B46-B48, B50,
     B53, B55, B57, B58.
W5e. 3 April 1919, Boston Symphony Orchestra, Sanders
     Theatre, Cambridge, Mass., Henri Rabaud, conductor.
W5f. 25 and 26 April 1919, Cincinnati Symphony Orchestra,
     Eugène Ysaye, conductor.
W5g. 17 and 18 October 1919, Philadelphia Orchestra,
     Leopold Stokowski, conductor. See B45.
W5h. 28 and 29 November 1919, St. Louis Symphony
     Orchestra, Max Zach, conductor.
W5i. 7 March 1920, Cleveland Orchestra, Nikolai Sokoloff,
     conductor. See B51.
W5j. 19 and 20 November 1920, Chicago Symphony Orchestra,
     Frederick Stock, conductor.
W5k. 18 December 1922, American Orchestral Society, New
     York, Chalmers Clifton, conductor.
W5m. 19 March 1923, Birmingham and Midland Institute
     Orchestral Concert, Granville Bantock, conductor.
W5n. 7 January 1934, People's Symphony, Boston, Fabien
     Sevitzky, conductor. See B54.
W5o. 4 January 1940, American Composers Concert, Kilbourn
     Hall, Rochester, N.Y., Rochester Civic Orchestra,
     Howard Hanson, conductor. Simultaneous radio
     broadcast on NBC.

W6. **Prelude to "The Trojan Women" of Euripides**, op. 25,
     1915 - Apr. 1920.

     4(picc).3(engh).5(bscl).3(cbsn) 6.3.3.0 perc, pf,
     hp, str.
     Part set, pencil score, and ink holograph in MH-H.

     Premiere:
W6a. Norfolk, Mass., June 1920.

W7. **The Fall of the House of Usher, Poem for Orchestra
     after Poe**, op. 27, Aug.- Sept. 1919.

     Duration 10'.
     3(picc).3(engh).3(bscl).0 4.4.3.1 timp, perc(4),
     cel, hp, str.
     Pencil draft in MH-H.

Premiere:
W7a. 29 and 30 October 1920, Boston Symphony Orchestra,
      Pierre Monteux, conductor. See H169, B62, B63, B65,
      B67, B68, B70.

Other Selected Performances:
W7b. 3 November 1920, Boston Symphony Orchestra, Lyric
      Theatre, Baltimore, Md., Pierre Monteux, conductor.
W7c. 6 November 1920, Boston Symphony Orchestra, Carnegie
      Hall, New York, N.Y., Pierre Monteux, conductor.
      See B64, B66, B69.
W7d. 11 November 1920, Boston Symphony Orchestra, Sanders
      Theatre, Cambridge, Mass., Pierre Monteux,
      conductor.

W8.   Nine Waltzes for Orchestra, op. 28, 1920.

      Duration 8'.
      3.3(engh).2.3(cbsn) 4.3.3.1 timp, perc(6), hp(2),
      glock, cel, str.
      Orchestrated version of W78.
      Part set and two ink holographs in MH-H.

      Premiere:
W8a. 24 and 25 February 1922, Boston Symphony Orchestra,
      Pierre Monteux, conductor. See B71-B77.

      Other Selected Performance:
W8b. 2 March 1922, Boston Symphony Orchestra, Sanders
      Theatre, Cambridge, Mass., Pierre Monteux,
      conductor.

W9.   March for King James' Entrance, Apr. 1921.

      Arranged for piano solo, W79.
      Pencil holograph in MH-H.

      Premiere:
W9a. 20 July 1921, at the Tercentenary celebration of
      Pilgrims' landing, Plymouth, Mass., Gallo Symphony
      Band, Chalmers Clifton, conductor. See B78-B80.

W10. Stevensoniana Suite, No. 2, After Poems from R. L.
      Stevenson's "A Child's Garden of Verses", op. 29,
      May 1921 - Sept. 1922. Schirmer, 1925.
      1. "Armies in the Fire"
      2. "The Dumb Soldier"
      3. "The Pirate Story"

      Duration 11'.
      3(picc).3(engh).3(bscl).3(cbsn) 4.2.3.1 timp,
      perc(5), cel, glock, hp, str.
      Movement 1 arranged for piano duet, W101.
      Two pencil and two ink holographs in MH-H.

Premiere:
W10a. 25 March 1923, New York Symphony Society, Walter
       Damrosch, conductor. See B81, B86, B87.

Other Selected Performances:
W10b. 21 and 22 March 1924, Boston Symphony Orchestra,
       Pierre Monteux, conductor. See H177, B83-B85.
W10c. 10 April 1924, Boston Symphony Orchestra, Sanders
       Theatre, Cambridge, Mass., Pierre Monteux,
       conductor.
W10d. 31 January and 1 February 1929, Los Angeles
       Philharmonic Orchestra, Georg Schnéevoigt,
       conductor. See B82.
W10e. 15 March 1934, New England Conservatory Orchestra
       (movement 3 only), Wallace Goodrich, conductor.
W10f. 16 and 18 January 1942, Pittsburgh Symphony Orchestra,
       Fritz Reiner, conductor.

W11. Lilacs, Poem for Orchestra, op. 33, 1926. Cos Cob
       Press, 1931.

       Duration 19'.
       3(picc).3(engh).3(bscl).3(cbsn) 6.3.3.1 timp,
       perc(3), cel, hp, pf, str.
       Dedication: "In Memoriam A[my] L[owell]"
       Arranged for piano duet, W113.
       Pencil holograph in NNAL.

       Premiere:
W11a. 31 March 1927, Boston Symphony Orchestra at Sanders
       Theatre in Cambridge, Mass., Serge Koussevitzky,
       conductor. See H170.

       Other Selected Performances:
W11b. 1 and 2 April 1927, Boston Symphony Orchestra, Serge
       Koussevitzky, conductor. See B99, B102, B108.
W11c. 5 April 1927, Boston Symphony Orchestra, Constitution
       Hall, Washington, D.C., Serge Koussevitzky,
       conductor.
W11d. 9 April 1927, Boston Symphony Orchestra, Carnegie
       Hall, New York, N.Y., Serge Koussevitzky, conductor.
       See B94, B96, B98, B100, B111.
W11e. 26 April 1927, Boston Symphony Orchestra, Serge
       Koussevitzky, conductor.
W11f. 1 May 1930, Boston Symphony Orchestra, Sanders
       Theatre, Cambridge, Mass., Serge Koussevitzky,
       conductor.
W11g. 2 and 3 May 1930, Boston Symphony Orchestra, Serge
       Koussevitzky, conductor. See B101, B106.
W11h. 4 October 1930, Boston Symphony Orchestra, Serge
       Koussevitzky, conductor.
W11i. 24 and 26 March 1932, Cleveland Orchestra, Nikolai
       Sokoloff, conductor. See B103.
W11j. 27 and 28 January 1934, St. Louis Symphony Orchestra,
       Vladimir Golschmann, conductor. See B95.
W11k. 29 and 30 November 1935, Boston Symphony Orchestra,
       Serge Koussevitzky, conductor. See B107, B109.

W11m. 16 January 1936, Boston Symphony Orchestra, Sanders
       Theatre, Cambridge, Mass., Serge Koussevitzky,
       conductor.
W11n. 7 May 1936, Brooklyn Symphony Orchestra, Manhatten
       Theatre, New York, N.Y., Chalmers Clifton,
       conductor.
W11o. 11 November 1936, Philadelphia Orchestra, American
       Academy of Arts and Letters Concert, Academy
       Auditorium, New York, N.Y., Henry Hadley,
       conductor.
W11p. 17 October 1937, Illinois Symphony Orchestra, Chicago,
       Ill.
W11q. 29 March 1939, Société des Concerts du Conservatoire,
       Grand Amphithéatre, Sorbonne, Charles Münch,
       conductor. See B97, B105.
W11r. 1 and 2 February 1940, Chicago Symphony Orchestra,
       Frederick Stock, conductor. See B104.
W11s. 17 and 18 April 1942, Boston Symphony Orchestra,
       Serge Koussevitzky, conductor. See B110, B112.
W11t. 30 April 1942, Boston Symphony Orchestra, Sanders
       Theatre, Cambridge, Mass., Serge Koussevitzky,
       conductor.
W11u. 21 and 23 February 1946, Cleveland Orchestra, Rudolph
       Ringwall, conductor.

W12.   Symphony in B-flat, op. 34, Jun.- Nov. 1927.
       Three movements.

       Duration 18'.
       4(picc).3(engh).4(bscl).3(cbsn) 6.4.3.1 timp,
       perc(5), glock, pf, str.
       Dedication: "To Sergei Koussevitzky"
       Arranged for piano duet, W104.
       Pencil draft, pencil holograph, ink holograph, and
       reproduction of holograph in MH-H (note: in draft
       stage entitled Three Symphonic Pieces); copyist's
       manuscript in DLC.

       Premiere:
W12a. 30 and 31 March 1928, Boston Symphony Orchestra,
       Serge Koussevitzky, conductor. See H178, B124,
       B125, B127, B132.

       Other Selected Performances:
W12b. 12 April 1928, Boston Symphony Orchestra, Carnegie
       Hall, New York, N.Y., Serge Koussevitzky, conductor.
       See B113, B114, B116, B117, B119, B121, B126, B129,
       B134, B136.
W12c. 19 April 1928, Boston Symphony Orchestra, Sanders
       Theatre, Cambridge, Mass., Serge Koussevitzky,
       conductor. See B123.
W12d. 22 and 23 March 1929, Boston Symphony Orchestra, Serge
       Koussevitzky, conductor.
W12e. 28 March 1929, Boston Symphony Orchestra, Sanders
       Theatre, Cambridge, Mass., Serge Koussevitzky,
       conductor.

W12f. 21 and 22 January, 1932, Chicago Symphony Orchestra,
      Frederick Stock, conductor. See B120.
W12g. 20 December 1934, Boston Symphony Orchestra, Sanders
      Theatre, Cambridge, Mass., Serge Koussevitzky,
      conductor.
W12h. 21 and 22 December 1934, Boston Symphony Orchestra,
      Richard Burgin, conductor.
W12i. 23 and 24 February 1939, Los Angeles Philharmonic
      Orchestra, Otto Klemperer, conductor. See B115,
      B122, B128, B130, B131, B135.
W12j. 26 and 27 February 1943, Boston Symphony Orchestra,
      Serge Koussevitzky, conductor. See B118, B133.

W13. Symphony No. 2, op. 35, Jul. 1929 - Feb. 1930.
      Four movements.

      Duration 24'.
      4(picc).3(engh).4(bscl).3(cbsn) 6.4.3.1 timp,
      perc(4), pf, str.
      Arranged for piano duet, W105.
      Dedication: "Dedicated to Walter R. Spalding"
      Pencil draft, ink holograph, and part set in MH-H.

      Premiere:
W13a. 27 and 28 February 1931, Boston Symphony Orchestra,
      Serge Koussevitzky, conductor. See H179, B147,
      B149, B150, B152.

      Other Selected Performances:
W13b. 7 March 1931, Boston Symphony Orchestra, Carnegie
      Hall, New York, N.Y., Serge Koussevitzky, conductor.
      See B151.
W13c. 12 March 1931, Boston Symphony Orchestra, Sanders
      Theatre, Cambridge, Mass., Serge Koussevitzky,
      conductor. See B148.

W14. Sinfonietta in One Movement for Orchestra, op. 37,
      Jun.- Nov. 1932.

      Duration 15'.
      4(picc).3(engh).4(bscl).3(cbsn) 6.3.3.1 timp,
      perc(6), pf, str.
      Pencil draft, pencil holograph, ink holograph, and
      part set in MH-H.

      Premiere:
W14a. 9 March 1933, Boston Symphony Orchestra, Sanders
      Theatre, Cambridge, Mass., Serge Koussevitzky,
      conductor. See H176, B180.

      Other Selected Performances:
W14b. 10 and 11 March 1933, Boston Symphony Orchestra,
      Serge Koussevitzky, conductor. See B174, B176,
      B177, B181, B183-B185.
W14c. 29 March 1933, Berlin Philharmonic, Fabien Sevitzky,
      conductor. See B175.

W14d. 23 and 24 April 1933, Concerts Pasdeloup, Théâtre des
       Champs Elysées, Paris, Fabien Sevitzky, conductor.
       See B178, B179, B182, B186.

W15. Two Jazz Studies, Nov. 1935 - May 1936.

       2.2.2.2 4.3.3.1 perc, pf, str.
       Orchestrated version of W102, nos. 2 and 4.
       Two ink holographs of no. 4, pencil holograph of no.
       4, and part sets of nos. 2 and 4 in MH-H.

       Premiere:
W15a. 20 May 1936, Boston Pops Orchestra, "Radcliffe Night,"
       Arthur Fiedler, conductor. See B198.

       Other Selected Performance:
W15b. 13 May 1940, Boston Pops Orchestra, "Harvard Night,"
       Benjamin Grosbayne, conductor.

W16. Sinfonietta for String Orchestra, op. 40a, 1936.
       Arrow Music Press, 1940.
       Four movements.

       Duration 16½'.
       Arrangement for string orchestra of W57.
       Dedication: "To Dr Serge Koussevitzky"

       Premiere:
W16a. 3 April 1936, Boston Symphony Orchestra, Brooklyn
       Academy of Music, Brooklyn, N.Y., Serge
       Koussevitzky, conductor. See B205, B233, B235,
       B242.

       Other Selected Performances:
W16b. 4 April 1936, Boston Symphony Orchestra at Carnegie
       Hall, New York, N.Y., Serge Koussevitzky, conductor.
       See B204, B212, B213, B218, B219, B224, B231, B237.
W16c. 17 and 18 April 1936, Boston Symphony Orchestra,
       Serge Koussevitzky, conductor. See B214, B225,
       B232, B234, B236, B239, B240, B244, B245, B247,
       B249.
W16d. 23 April 1936, Boston Symphony Orchestra, Sanders
       Theatre, Cambridge, Mass., Serge Koussevitzky,
       conductor.
W16e. 19 June 1936, Boston Opera House (finale only),
       Commonwealth Symphony Orchestra, Alexander Theide,
       conductor. See B238.
W16f. 16 September 1936, Harvard Tercentenary Concert,
       Harvard University (middle two movements only),
       Boston Symphony Orchestra, Serge Koussevitzky,
       conductor. See B211, B216, B221, B251.
W16g. 11 and 13 March 1937, Cleveland Orchestra, Rudolph
       Ringwall, conductor.
W16h. 7 August 1937, Berkshire Symphonic Music Festival,
       Boston Symphony Orchestra, Serge Koussevitzky,
       conductor. See B227, B230, B243, B246.

W16i. 6 December 1937, Boston Chamber String Orchestra,
      Boston City Club.
W16j. 2 and 3 February 1940, St. Louis Symphony Orchestra,
      Vladimir Golschmann, conductor. See B208, B209,
      B220, B228.
W16k. 23 and 24 February 1940, Philadelphia Orchestra,
      Eugene Ormandy, conductor. See B223, B226, B241.
W16m. 27 February 1940, Philadelphia Orchestra, Constitution
      Hall, Washington, D.C., Eugene Ormandy, conductor.
      See B206, B207, B215, B217.
W16n. 28 February 1940, Philadelphia Orchestra, Lyric
      Theatre, Baltimore, Md., Eugene Ormandy, conductor.
      See B210, B229, B248.
W16o. 26 April 1944, Festival of American Music, Kilbourn
      Hall, Rochester, N.Y., Eastman Little Symphony,
      Paul White, conductor. See B222.

W17. Symphony No. 3, op. 41, Aug. 1936 - Mar. 1937.
      Three movements.

      Duration 28'.
      4(picc).3(engh).3.3(cbsn) 4.3.3.1 timp, perc(5), pf,
      str.
      Arranged for piano duet, W108.
      Two pencil drafts, pencil holograph, ink holograph,
      and part set in MH-H.

      Premiere:
W17a. 3 and 4 December 1937, Boston Symphony Orchestra,
      Serge Koussevitzky, conductor. See H180, B252,
      B254, B256, B258-B266, B268.

      Other Selected Performances:
W17b. 16 December 1937, Boston Symphony Orchestra, Sanders
      Theatre, Cambridge, Mass., Serge Koussevitzky,
      conductor.
W17c. 23 and 25 February 1939, Cleveland Orchestra, Artur
      Rodzinski, conductor. See B253, B255, B257, B267.

W18. The Flute, Poem for Orchestra after the Story by
      Marcel Schwob, op. 45, Jul.- Nov. 1939.

      3.3(engh).3(bscl).3(cbsn) 6.3.3.1 timp, perc, pf,
      str.
      Pencil draft, pencil holograph, part set, and ink
      holograph in MH-H.

W19. Concertino [or Sinfonietta] for String Orchestra,
      op. 46, Aug.- Sep. 1939.
      Three movements.

      Duration 16'.
      Arranged for piano duet, W110.
      Two pencil drafts, pencil holograph, ink manuscript
      by copyist, and part set in MH-H.

Premiere:
W19a. 19 and 20 April 1940, Boston Symphony Orchestra, Serge
      Koussevitzky, conductor. See B298-B306.

W20.   Symphony No. 4, op. 47, Jul. 1940 - Jul. 1941.
          Three movements.

       Arranged for piano duet, W115.
       Pencil draft, pencil holograph, and ink holograph in
          MH-H.

W21.   Suite for String Orchestra, Nov. 1945 - May 1946.
          Four movements.

       Duration 12'.
       Pencil holograph in MH-H.

W22.   Diversion for Small Orchestra, Apr.- May 1947.

       Duration 15'.
       Pencil draft and ink holograph in MH-H.

W23.   Four Pieces for String Orchestra, Aug. 1947 -
          Apr. 1948.
          1. "Overture"
          2. "Air"
          3. "Minuet"
          4. "Jig"

       Orchestral arrangement of W111.
       Pencil draft and pencil holograph in MH-H.

W24.   Prelude for Orchestra, Dec. 1952 - Jan. 1953.

       Duration 6'.
       2.2.3.2 2.2.3.0 timp, perc, pf, str.
       Commissioned by the Koussevitzky Music Foundation.
       Dedication: "In Memoriam Serge and Natalie
          Koussevitzky"
       Pencil draft and pencil holograph in MH-H;
          reproductions of holograph in DLC.
       See D2, B324-B328.

       Premiere:
W24a. 29 March 1953, Koussevitzky Music Foundation Tenth
          Anniversary Concert, Town Hall, New York, N.Y.,
          Leonard Bernstein, conductor. See B312, B313, B315.

       Other Selected Performance:
W24b. 21, 22, 23 October 1975, Oakland Symphony, Paramount
          Theater, Oakland, Calif., Harold Farberman,
          conductor. See B314, B316.

W25.   A Siesta, n.d.

Pencil holograph in MH-H.

Works for Solo Instrument(s) with Orchestra

W26.   Humoresque, Waltz, Quasi Fox Trot for Clarinet and
Small Orchestra, Jun.- Jul. 1920.

Orchestrated version of W50.
Pencil and ink holographs in MH-H.

W27.   Scherzo for Two Pianos and Orchestra, Apr. 1923 -
Aug. 1924.

Duration 12'.
3(picc).2.2.2   4.2.3.1   timp, perc(6), glock, pf(2),
str.
Dedication: "To Guy Marco and Lee Pattison"
Pencil and ink holographs in MH-H.

Premiere:
W27a.   19 and 20 December 1924, Boston Symphony Orchestra,
Serge Koussevitzky, conductor; Guy Marco and Lee
Pattison, soloists.   See H175, B88-B92.

W28.   Divertimento for Piano and Orchestra, Jul.- Aug. 1926.

3(picc).3(engh).2.3(cbsn)   4.2.3.1   timp, perc, str.
Arranged for piano duet, W103.
Dedication: "To Chalmers Clifton"
Copyist's manuscript and part set in MH-H.

Premiere:
W28a.   28 March 1927, American Orchestral Society, Aeolian
Hall, New York, N.Y., Chalmers Clifton, conductor;
Katherine Bacon, soloist.   See B93.

W29.   Concertino in One Movement for Piano and Orchestra,
op. 36, Jul.- Aug. 1931.

Duration 12'.
3(picc).3(engh).2.2   4.3.3.1   timp, perc(5), pf, str.
Arranged for piano duet, W107.
Dedication: "To Jesús Mariá Sanromá"
Ink holograph in possession of Mrs. Mercedes P.
Sanromá; pencil draft, pencil holograph, and two
reproductions of ink holograph in MH-H; one
reproduction of holograph in MBCM.

Premiere:
W29a. 25 April 1932, Boston Symphony Orchestra, Serge
        Koussevitzky, conductor; Jesús Mariá Sanromá,
        soloist. See H168, B162, B165, B168-B171.

Other Selected Performances:
W29b. 28 April 1932, Boston Symphony Orchestra, Sanders
        Theatre, Cambridge, Mass., Serge Koussevitzky,
        conductor; Jesús Mariá Sanromá, soloist. See B164.
W29c. 4 May 1933, Festival of American Music, Eastman
        Theatre, Rochester, New York, Rochester Philharmonic
        Orchestra, Howard Hanson, conductor; Sandor Vas,
        soloist. See B153, B157, B158, B173.
W29d. 19 November 1933, New Haven Symphony Orchestra,
        Woolsey Hall, David Stanley Smith, conductor; Edwin
        Gorschefski, soloist. See B159, B167.
W29e. 31 January 1934, Boston Symphony Orchestra, Lyric
        Theatre, Baltimore, Md., Serge Koussevitzky,
        conductor; Jesús Mariá Sanromá, soloist.
W29f. 1 February 1934, Boston Symphony Orchestra, Brooklyn
        Academy of Music, Brooklyn, N.Y., Serge
        Koussevitzky, conductor; Jesús Mariá Sanromá,
        soloist. See B154, B155.
W29g. 3 February 1934, Boston Symphony Orchestra, Carnegie
        Hall, New York, N.Y., Serge Koussevitzky, conductor;
        Jesús Mariá Sanromá, soloist. See B156, B160, B166.
W29h. 9 and 10 March 1934, Boston Symphony Orchestra, Serge
        Koussevitzky, conductor; Jesús Mariá Sanromá,
        soloist. See B161, B163, B172.

W30.   Romance for Violin and Orchestra, Sep. 1931.

       Arranged for violin and piano, W69.
       Pencil draft, pencil holograph, and ink holograph
         (incomp.) in MH-H; ink holograph and two parts in
         MBCM.

W31.   Concerto for Violin and Orchestra, op. 38, Jul. 1933 -
         Feb. 1934 (rev. 1937).
         Three movements.

       Duration 25'.
       2.2.3(bscl).3(cbsn) 4.2.3.1 timp, perc(3), str.
       Arranged for violin and piano, W55.
       Pencil draft, pencil holograph, ink holograph,
         copyist's manuscript, and part set in MH-H.

       Premiere:
W31a. 11 and 12 November 1938, Boston Symphony Orchestra,
        Serge Koussevitzky, conductor; Ruth Posselt,
        soloist. See B276, B279, B286, B289-B294, B297.

       Other Selected Performances:
W31b. 12 March 1939, National Symphony Orchestra, Hans

Kindler, conductor; Ruth Posselt, soloist. See
        B277, B278, B282, B296.
W31c. 16 November 1939, Boston Symphony Orchestra, Sanders
        Theatre, Cambridge, Mass., Serge Koussevitzky,
        conductor; Ruth Posselt, soloist. See B281.
W31d. 24 November 1939, Boston Symphony Orchestra, Brooklyn
        Academy of Music, Brooklyn, N.Y., Serge
        Koussevitzky, conductor; Ruth Posselt, soloist. See
        B283, B284.
W31e. 25 November 1939, Boston Symphony Orchestra, Carnegie
        Hall, New York, N.Y., Serge Koussevitzky,
        conductor; Ruth Posselt, soloist. See B275, B280,
        B285, B287, B288, B295.

W32.   Concertino, No. 2, for Piano and Orchestra, op. 44,
        Aug. 1938 - Apr. 1939.

        Arranged for piano duet, W109.
        Two pencil drafts, two pencil holographs, and ink
        holograph in MH-H.

W33.   Music for English Horn and Orchestra, op. 50, Apr.-
        Oct. 1943.

        Duration 8'.
        Dedication: "To Louis Speyer"
        Pencil and ink holographs in MH-H.

        Premiere:
W33a. 2 and 3 March 1945, Boston Symphony Orchestra, Serge
        Koussevitzky, conductor; Louis Speyer, soloist. See
        H171, B307-B309, B311.

        Other Selected Performances:
W33b. 7 and 8 January 1949, Boston Symphony Orchestra, Serge
        Koussevitzky, conductor; Louis Speyer, soloist.
W33c. 15 January 1949, Boston Symphony Orchestra, Carnegie
        Hall, New York, N.Y., Serge Koussevitzky, conductor;
        Louis Speyer, soloist. See B310.

W34.   Lyric Piece for Violincello and Orchestra, op. 51,
        May-Nov. 1943.

        Pencil draft, pencil holograph, and ink holograph in
        MH-H.
        n.b. Quintet for Clarinet and String Quartet, W62,
        also labelled op. 51.

W35.   Concertino for Two Flutes and Small Orchestra, Oct.-
        Dec. 1947

        Two pencil drafts and pencil holograph in MH-H.

Music for Dance and Pantomime

W36.   Jack Frost in Mid-Summer, Pantomime for Orchestra,
          op. 16, 1908.

          Scenario by Joseph Lindon Smith.
          "Moth Dance" arranged for piano duet, W99.
          Ink draft, pencil holograph, copyist's manuscript, and
          part set in MH-H.

          Premiere:
W36a. 6 January 1908, Chicago Symphony Orchestra, Frederick
          Stock, conductor. See B28.

W37.   Pan and the Star, Pantomime for Orchestra and Women's
          Voices, op. 19, 1914.

          3(picc).3(engh).3(bscl).3 4.3.3.1 timp, perc, hp,
          str.
          Scenario by Joseph Lindon Smith.
          Pencil holograph and part set in MH-H; ink holograph
          in DLC.

          Premiere:
W37a. 21 August 1914, MacDowell Festival, Peterborough,
          N.H., Chalmers Clifton, conductor. See B35, B36.

          Other Selected Performance:
W37b. 8 December 1914, Boston, Chalmers Clifton, conductor.

W38.   Pantomime Sketches for "The Silence of the Harp" for
          Piano, 1917.

          Scenario by Joseph Lindon Smith.
          Three ink holographs in MH-H.

Musical Drama

W39.   Granada, or the Sorcerer, the Soubrette and the
          Showman, Hasty Pudding Club Play, Harvard
          University, 1894. Miles and Thompson, 1894.

          Collaboration with Daniel Gregory Mason.
          Ink holograph of the duet "Mirzah and Minstrel" in
          MH-H.

          Premiere:
W39a. 12, 13, and 14 April 1894 (two performances on the
          14th), Copley Hall, Cambridge, Mass., Hasty Pudding
          Club members. See B27.

Music for Solo Voice and Orchestra

W40.   Romance for Baritone and Orchestra, op. 17, n.d.
           (?between 1908 [op. 16] and 1914 [op. 19]).

           Text by Dante Gabriel Rossetti.
           Ink holograph in MH-H.

W41.   Autumn Twilight for Soprano and Orchestra, op. 21,
           n.d. (?between 1913 [op. 20] and 1915 [op. 22]).

           3(picc).3(engh).3(bscl).2 4.2.3.1 timp, perc, hp,
               str.
           Text by Arthur Symons.
           Arranged for soprano and piano duet, W152.
           Pencil draft and ink holograph in MH-H.

W42.   Three Songs Without Text With Orchestral
           Accompaniment, Jul. 1939 - Oct. 1948.

           Orchestrated version of W142.
           2.2.2.1 4.2.0.0 hp, str.
           Dedication: "To Doris Doe"
           Pencil draft, pencil holograph, and part set in MH-H;
               ink holograph (piano-vocal score) in MBCM.

W43.   The Ballad of Sir Guy for Voice and Orchestra, n.d.

           Text by Henry Copley Greene.
           Copyist's manuscript in MH-H.

Choral Music

W44.   Nuns of the Perpetual Adoration, for chorus and
           orchestra, op. 15, 1906-08. Boston Music Co., 1909,
           piano-vocal score.

           Duration 16'.
           3(picc).2.2.2 4.3.3.1 timp, perc, hp, str.
           Text by Ernest Dowson.
           Pencil-ink holograh, two ink holographs, and part set
               in MH-H.

           Premiere:
W44a. 18 May 1909, American Music Society Concert, Jordan
           Hall, Boston, Choral Club of the New England

Conservatory (with piano only), George W. Chadwick, conductor, Genevieve Baker, piano. See B30, B33.

Other Selected Performances:
W44b. 24 April 1911, Musical Art Club, Jordan Hall, Boston, Chalmers Clifton, conductor.
W44c. 18 May 1911, American Music Society, Boston, George W. Chadwick, conductor.
W44d. May 1911, Midland Institute, Birmingham, England, Granville Bantock, conductor.
W44e. 13 February 1914, Modern Music Society, Aeolian Hall, New York, N.Y., Benjamin Lambord, conductor. See B32.
W44f. 24 June 1934, Choral Society of the Massachusetts Federation of Women's Clubs, All Saints Church, Peterborough, N.H., George Sawyer Dunham, conductor; Reginald Boardman, piano.
W44g. 7 April 1936, MacDowell Club Orchestra and Chorus, Jordan Hall, Boston, Arthur Fiedler, conductor. See B29, B31, B34.

W45. <u>Music, When Soft Voices Die</u>, for women's voices, unaccompanied, Mar. 1911.

Text by Percy B. Shelley.
Ink holograph in MH-H.

W46. <u>And the Wilderness Shall Rejoice</u>, for chorus and organ, 1915. Boston Music Co., c. 1915, piano-vocal score.

Dedication: "Anthem for the Centenary Celebration of Allegheny College"
Pencil and ink holographs in MH-H.

Premiere:
W46a. 21 June 1915, Allegheny College Centenary Commemoration, Meadville, Penn.

W47. <u>Ode for Mixed Chorus and Orchestra</u>, Jun.- Aug. 1930.

Duration 15'.
4.3(engh).4(bscl).3(cbsn) 6.3.3.1 timp, perc(4), pf, str.
Dedication: "For the fiftieth anniversary of the Boston Symphony Orchestra"
Text by Robert Hillyer.
Pencil draft, pencil holograph, and choral parts in MH-H.

Premiere:
W47a. 17 and 18 October 1930, Boston Symphony Orchestra, Harvard Glee Club, Radcliffe Choral Society, Serge Koussevitzky, conductor. See H173, B140-B146.

Chamber Music

W48. Pastorale for String Quartet, 1892.

      Ink holograph in MH-H.

W49. Quartet in A minor for Strings, op. 26, 1918.
         Four movements.

      Ink holograph in MH-H.

W50. Humoresque, Waltz, and Quasi Fox Trot for Clarinet and
         Piano, Aug.- Oct. 1919.

      Arranged for clarinet and orchestra, W26.
      Ink holograph in MH-H.

W51. Idyl, Elegy, and Scherzo for Flute and Piano, Dec.
         1921 - Jan. 1922.

      Ink holograph in MH-H.

W52. Sonata for Flute and Piano, op. 31, Jun.- Aug. 1925.

      Dedication: "To Georges Laurent"
      Pencil holograph and ink holograph in MH-H; ink
         holograph of second movement in OCU.

      Selected Performance:
W52a. 10 May 1940, All-Hill Concert in honor of his
         retirement, Paine Hall, Harvard University, George
         Laurent and Jesús Mariá Sanromá.

W53. Sonata for Clarinet (or Violin) and Piano, op. 32,
         Aug. 1925 - Jan. 1926. Society for the Publication
         of American Music, 1927.
         Three movements.

      Dedication: "For Paul Mimart"
      Ink holograph in MH-H.

      Selected Performance:
W53a. 12 March 1939, Recital sponsored by the National
         Association for American Composers and Conductors,
         New York, N.Y., Arthur Christmann, clarinet; Harold
         Morris, piano.

W54.   Four Pieces for Wind Instruments, Aug.- Sep. 1928.
          1. "Prelude"
          2. "Quasi Minuetto"
          3. "Scherzino"
          4. "Elegy"

       Ink holograph in MH-H.

       Premiere:
W54a. 20 January 1929, Boston Flute Players' Club, Boston
          Art Club, Boston, George Laurent, flute; Gaston
          Hamelin and Paul Mimart, clarinet; George Bottcher,
          horn. See B137, B139.

       Other Selected Performance:
W54b. 25 April 1929, Boston Wind Ensemble, Paine Hall,
          Harvard University, George Laurent, flute; Gaston
          Hamelin and Paul Mimart, clarinet; Willem Valkenier,
          horn. See B138.

W55.   Arrangement of Concerto for Violin and Orchestra for
          violin and piano, 1933.

       Arrangement of W31.
       Four pencil holographs, four ink holographs, and two
       copyist's manuscripts MH-H.

W56.   Sextet for Flute, Oboe, Clarinet, Horn, Bassoon, and
          Piano, op. 39, Jun.- Aug. 1934. Galaxy Music, 1939.
          Four movements.

       Commissioned by Elizabeth Sprague Coolidge.
       Ink holograph in DLC; pencil holograph in MH-H.
       See D3, B317-323.

       Premiere:
W56a. 20 September 1934, Berkshire Music Festival,
          Pittsfield, Mass., Jesús Mariá Sanromá, piano, and
          the Laurent Wind Quintet. See B190, B192, B193,
          B196, B197.

       Other Selected Performances:
W56b. 17 July 1937, Festival of Pan American Chamber Music,
          in Mexico City, sponsored by Elizabeth Sprague
          Coolidge.
W56c. 27 April 1944, Festival of American Music, Rochester,
          N.Y. See B194.
W56d. 19 May 1950, Festival of Contemporary Music,
          sponsored by the Alice M. Ditson Fund of Columbia
          University and the American Academy and National
          Institute of Arts and Letters, MacMillan Theatre,
          Columbia University, New York, N.Y., Joseph Seiger,
          piano, and the Five-Wind Ensemble. See B187-B189,
          B191, B195.

W57.   Quartet for Strings, op. 40, Jul.- Sep. 1935 (rev.
        Sep. 1951).
        Four movements.

        Arranged for orchestra, W16.
        Dedication: "To Yves Chardon and the Chardon Quartet"
        Pencil holograph in MH-H; ink holograph, copyist's
        manuscript, and part set in MBCM.

        Premiere:
W57a.   23 January 1936, Chardon Quartet, Paine Hall, Harvard
        University. See B199.

        Other Selected Performances:
W57b.   16 September 1936, Harvard Tercentenary Concert,
        Paine Hall, Harvard University, Chardon String
        Quartet. See B201-B203.
W57c.   10 May 1940, All-Hill Concert in honor of his
        retirement, Paine Hall, Harvard University, Chardon
        String Quartet. See B200.
W57d.   1 May 1943, Boston String Quartet, Paine Hall, Harvard
        University.

W58.   Quartet for Piano and Strings, op. 42, Jun.- Sep.
        1937.
        Four movements.

        Two pencil holographs in MH-H; score (part
        holograph), part set, and copyist's manuscript of
        score in MBCM.

        Premiere:
W58a.   11 January 1938, Jesús Mariá Sanromá, piano, and the
        Boston String Quartet, Jordan Hall, Boston. See
        B269-B274.

W59.   Sonata for Two Clarinets in B-flat, op. 43, Jul. -
        Aug. 1938.
        Three movements.

        Ink holograph in MH-H.

W60.   Trio for Clarinet, Cello, and Piano, op. 48, 1941-42.
        Four movements.

        Pencil holograph in MH-H; ink holograph and part set
        (by copyist) in MBCM

W61.   Sonata for Two Clarinets, op. 49, 1942.
        Three movements.

        Pencil holograph in MH-H.

W62. <u>Quintet for Clarinet and String Quartet</u>, op. 51,
      Sep. 1944 - Apr. 1945.
      Four movements.

      Pencil draft, ink holographs, and reproductions of
      parts in MH-H.
      n.b. <u>Lyric Piece for Cello and Orchestra</u>, W34, also
      labelled op. 51.

W63. <u>Three Pieces for Flute and Clarinet</u>, Sep. 1946.

      Pencil holograph in MH-H.

W64. <u>Sonata for Bassoon and Piano</u>, 1946-1948.
      Three movements

      Ink holograph in MH-H.

W65. <u>Sonatina for Cello and Piano</u>, Sep.- Nov. 1949.
      Three movements.

      Pencil drafts and ink holograph in MH-H.

W66. <u>Quintet for Piano and Strings</u>, begun Jun. 1950.
      Left unfinished.

      Pencil holograph in MH-H.

W67. <u>Sonatina for Violin and Piano</u>, Jul.- Sep. 1951.
      Three movements.

      Dedication: "For Alexander Bloch"
      Pencil and ink holographs in MH-H.

W68. <u>Sonatina for Clarinet and Piano</u>, Jul.- Oct. 1952.
      Three movements.

      Dedication: "To B[urnet] C[ouoin] T[uthill]"
      Holograph in DLC; Pencil and ink holographs in MH-H.

W69. Arrangement of <u>Romance for Violin and Orchestra</u> for
      violin and piano, n.d.

      Arrangement of W30.
      Ink holograph (incomp.) in MH-H.

W70. <u>Piece for Violincello and Piano</u>, n.d.

      Dedication: "For Mrs. Truman Fassett"
      Reproduction of ink holograph in MH-H.

Music for Solo Piano

W71. Sonata in F# minor for Pianoforte, 1894.
         Four movements.

         Dedication: "To D[aniel] G[regory] M[ason] in
            appreciation of his advice and sympathy"
         Ink holograph in MH-H.
         Note on holograph: "Awarded Summa cum Laude, Harvard
            University June 1894"

W72. Sketches, Nos. 1-5, after Stephen Crane, op. 7, 1895.

         Pencil and ink holographs in MH-H; ink holograph of
            no. 1 in DLC.
         n.b. Jazz Studies for Two Pianos, W102, also labelled
            op. 7.

         Selected Performance:
W72a. 18 May 1909, American Music Society Concert (no. 1
         only), Jordan Hall, Boston.

W73. Study, 1898.

         Pencil and ink holographs in MH-H; ink holograph in
         MBCM (entitled Etude).

W74. Three Poetical Sketches for Piano, op. 8, 1899.
         Breitkopf und Härtel, 1902.
         1. "Moonlight"
         2. "A Midsummer Lullaby"
         3. "From a Mountain Top"

         No. 1 reprinted in The Art of Music, ed. Daniel
            Gregory Mason, assoc. eds. E. B. Hill and Leland
            Hall, 14 vols. (New York: National Society of
            Music, 1915-17), 14:286-287.
         Ink holograph of no. 1 in NRU-Mus.
         Pencil and ink holographs in MH-H of six piano pieces
            entitled:
            1. "Moonlight"
            2. "Sunrise"
            3. "Sunset"
            4. "Night"
            5. "A Midsummer Lullaby"
            6. "From a Mountain Top"

W75. Country Idylls, Six Pieces for Piano, op. 10, 1900-01.
        Schirmer, 1903.
        1. "A Spring Morning"
        2. "A Starlit Night"
        3. "An Autumn Hunting Song"
        4. "An August Lullaby"
        5. "In a Garden by Moonlight"
        6. "A Summer Evening"

        Pencil and ink holographs in MH-H of two incomplete
        sets entitled:
        1. "A Spring Morning"
        2. "Mid-Summer Echoes"
        3. "At this Frolic"
        4. "An August Lullaby"

        3. "By a Mountain Brook"
        4. "An August Lullaby"
        5. "In a Garden of Moonlight"
        6. "A Summer Evening"

W76. At the Grave of a Hero, 1903. Wa-Wan Press, 1903;
        reprint ed., New York: Arno Press and the New York
        Times, 1970, vol. 2, pp. 51-53.

W77. Minuet, 1913.

        Dedication: "For A[lison] B[ixby] H[ill]"
        Ink holograph in MH-H.

W78. Nine Waltzes, op. 28, 1920. Nos. 3, 4, and 2
        published as Trois valses pour le piano in the
        "Supplément Musical du 1er Avril 1922" of Revue
        musicale 3/6 (1922).

        Arranged for orchestra, W8.

W79. March for King James' Entrance, 1921.

        Arrangement of W9.
        Two ink holographs in MH-H.

W80. Study for Piano, May-Jun. 1936.

        Originally entitled Design.
        Two ink holographs in MH-H.

W81. Lullaby for Millicent and Her Mother, Jan. 1942.

        Pencil holograph in MH-H.

W82.   Prelude, Toccatina, and Scherzino for Piano, Jan.
       1943.

       Two ink holographs in MH-H; ink holograph of Prelude
       and Scherzino in MBCM; ink holograph of Prelude and
       Toccatina in OCU.

W83.   Quasi Polonaise for Piano, Feb. 1943.

       Two ink holographs in MH-H; ink holograph in MBCM; ink
       holograph in OCU.

W84.   Etude (moto perpetuo), Feb. 1943.

       Pencil holograph in MH-H; ink holograph in MBCM.

W85.   Etude, Jul. 1943.

       Dedication: "For Dr. Ilse Hübner"
       Pencil and ink holographs in MH-H; ink holograph in
       OCU.

W86.   Chimes, Mar. 1944.

       Pencil and ink holographs in MH-H; two ink holographs
       in OCU.

W87.   Valser Scherzoso, 1946-48.

       Dedication: "To Miss Amie Endicott Nourse"
       Ink holograph in MH-H.

W88.   Bagatelle for Piano, Jul.- Nov. 1948.

       Dedication: "For George L. Foote"
       Ink holograph and two pencil holographs in MH-H.

W89.   Toccata, Dec. 1949.

       Two pencil holographs in MH-H.

W90.   Impromptu, May 1953.

       Dedication: "For Louise Millard"
       Pencil and ink holographs in MH-H.

W91.   Toccata giocosa, Aug. 1953.

       Two pencil and one ink holograph in MH-H.

W92.   3 Line Piece for Esther Hill, n.d.

Ink holograph in MH-H.

W93.   Four Spanish Songs Transcribed for Piano, n.d.
        1. "Lullaby"
        2. "Sequedillas"
        3. "Estudiantes"
        4. "A los Toros"

Ink holograph in MH-H.

W94.   Pastorale Scarlatti-Tausig, n.d.

Two ink holographs in MH-H.

W95.   Quasi Minuetto, n.d.

Dedication: "For Amie Endicott Nourse"
Two ink holographs in MH-H; ink holograph in OCU.

W96.   Quasi Sarabanda, n.d.

Ink holograph in MBCM.

W97.   Sonata No. 2 for Pianoforte after Kipling's "Light
        that Failed", n.d.
        1. [no title]
        2. "The Queen can do no wrong"
        3. "Finale"

Ink holograph in MH-H.

W98.   Sonata No. 4, n.d. (Sketch only)

Pencil sketch in MH-H.

Music for Piano Duet

W99.   Arrangement of the "Moth Dance" from Jack Frost in
        Midsummer for one piano, four hands, Feb. 1908.

Arrangement of one number from W36.
Ink holograph in MH-H.

W100. '94 Fox Trot, 1919.

Dedication: "Composed for the 25th Anniversary Dinner
[of the Class of 1894]"
Ink holograph in MH-H.

W101. Arrangement of first movement of Stevensoniana Suite,
No.2, "Armies in the Fire," for one piano, four
hands, Oct. 1922.

Arrangement of W10, no. 1.
Ink holograph in MH-H.

W102. Jazz Studies for Two Pianos, op. 7, c.1922-1936.   Nos.
1-4 published by Schirmer, c.1924-35.

Nos. 2 and 4 arranged for orchestra, W15.
No. 5, Dedication: "To Edward Ballantine"
Pencil and ink drafts and ink holographs in MH-H.
n.b. Sketches after Stephen Crane, W72, also labelled
op. 7.

Selected Performance:
W102a. 7 March 1942, Concert at the Teatro Santa Isabel,
Estelita Gonçalves and Alberto de Figueinedo,
pianists.

W103. Arrangement of Divertimento for Piano and Orchestra
for two pianos, 1926.

Arrangement of W28.
Pencil draft and two ink copyist's manuscripts in
MH-H.

W104. Arrangement of Symphony in B-flat for one piano, four
hands, 1927.

Arrangement of W12.
Ink holograph in MH-H.

W105. Arrangement of Symphony No. 2 for one piano, four
hands, 1929.

Arrangement of W13.
Ink holograph in MH-H.

W106. Synthetic Jazz, Jun. 1929.

Dedication: "Composed for the thirty-fifth anniversary
of the Class of 1894"
Ink holograph in MH-H.

W107. Arrangement of <u>Concertino in One Movement for Piano and Orchestra</u> for two pianos, 1931.

Arrangment of W29.
Ink holograph in MH-H.

W108. Arrangement of <u>Symphony No. 3</u> for one piano, four hands, 1936-37.

Arrangement of W17.
Ink holograph in MH-H.

W109. Arrangement of <u>Concertino, No. 2, for Piano and Orchestra</u> for two pianos, 1939.

Arrangement of W32.
Ink holograph in MH-H.

Premiere:
W109a. 10 May 1940, All-Hill Concert in honor of his retirement, Paine Hall, Harvard University, Walter Piston and Jesús Mariá Sanromá, pianists.

W110. Arrangement of <u>Concertino for String Orchestra</u> for one piano, four hands, 1939.

Arrangement of W19.
Ink holograph score in MH-H.

W111. <u>Four Pieces for Four Hands</u>, 1947.
        1. "Overture"
        2. "Air"
        3. "Minuet"
        4. "Jig"

Dedication of no. 1: "For Mrs. Arnold Weeks"
Arranged for string orchestra, W23.
Pencil holograph of no. 2, two pencil holographs of no. 4, and two ink holographs of no. 1 in MH-H.

W112. <u>Nocturne</u>, Oct.- Dec. 1949.

Pencil score in MH-H.

W113. Arrangement of <u>Lilacs</u> for one piano, four hands, n.d.

Arrangement of W11.
Ink holograph in MH-H.

W114. Preludes to Scenes 1, 2, and 3 of <u>Monaduock Invaded</u>, n.d.

Ink holograph in MH-H.

W115. Arrangement of <u>Symphony No. 4</u> for one piano, four hands, n.d.

Arrangement of W20.
Ink holograph in MH-H.

W116. <u>Two Pieces for Piano, Three and Four Hands</u>, n.d.
1. "Quasi Berceuse"
2. "Quasi Minuetto"

Dedication: "To Esther M. Hill"
Ink holograph in OCU.

Music for Solo Voice and Piano

W117. "River Song," 1894.

Text by Henry Copley Greene.
Ink holograph in MH-H.

W118. "Danser la Gigue," Jul. 1896.

Pencil holograph in MH-H.

W119. "All's Well," 1897.

Text by Henry Copley Greene.
Ink holograph in MH-H.

W120. "Pierre de Provence to Magnelme the Fair," 1898.

Text by Henry Copley Green.
Two ink holographs in MH-H.

W121. <u>Five Songs from the "Round Rabbit"</u>, op. 5, ?1897-
?1898. Boston: A. P. Schmidt, 1900.
1. "Watching for Sleep"
2. "The Moon in the Pond" (composed Mar. 1897)
3. "O Roundy Moon"
4. "Vanished June"
5. "Lullaby" (composed Dec. 1898)

Texts by Agnes Lee.

Ink holograph of nos. 1, 2, 3, 5 and pencil drafts of
no. 1 and 3 in MH-H.

W122. <u>Five Songs</u>, op. 6, ?1899. Breitkopf und Härtel, 1900.
1. "She Sat and Sang Alway"
2. "To Sleep, to Sleep"
3. "Ah! had I Thee but Sooner Seen"
4. "The Surges Gushed and Sounded" (composed May
   1899)
5. "The Full Sea Rolls and Thunders"

Text of no. 1 by Christina Rossetti; text of no. 2 by
Alfred Lord Tennyson; text of no. 4 by W. E. Henley.
Pencil holograph of no. 2 and 4 and ink holograph of
no. 1, 2, and 4 in MH-H.

W123. "When Lovely Woman Stoops to Folk," Apr. 1900.

Text by Oliver Goldsmith.
Pencil and ink holographs in MH-H.

W124. "Song for Contralto" ("The Flush Flies Far from the
Northwind's Breath"), Jan. 1901.

Text by Henry Copley Greene.
Ink holograph in MH-H.

W125. "In Kensington Gardens," op. 13, no.1; "Peace at
Noon," op. 13, no.2, Apr. 1904.

Texts by Arthur Symons.
Ink holographs in MH-H.

W126. "Spring Twilight," Nov. 1904.

Text by Arthur Symons.
Ink holograph in MH-H.

W127. "Fill a Glass with Golden Wine," Mar. 1905.

Text by W. E. Henley.
Pencil score in MH-H.

W128. "Scentless Gloves I Buy Thee," Mar. 1906 (rev. 1908).

Text by William Watson.
Ink holograph in MH-H.

W129. "Sweet and Low," 1907 (rev. 1908).

Text by G. Tennyson.
Ink holograph in MH-H.

W130. "The Splendor Falls on Castle Walls," 1907.

Text by G. Tennyson.
Ink holograph in MH-H.

W131. "The Owl," Mar. 1907.

Text by G. Tennyson.
Ink holograph in MH-H.

W132. "Beside the Idle Summer Sea," Mar. 1907.

Text by W. E. Henley.
Two ink holographs in MH-H.

W133. Venetian Nights, Apr. 1907.
    1. "Venata Marina"
    2. "At the Dogana"

Pencil holograph of no. 1 and ink holographs of no. 1
    and 2 in MH-H.

W134. "After Sunset," Apr. 1907.

Text by Arthur Symons.
Pencil holograph in MH-H.

W135. "From an Old French Song Book," Jul. 1907.

Trans. by Arthur Symons.
Three ink holographs in MH-H; copyist's manuscript in
    MBCM.

W136. Fêtes galantes by Paul Verlaine, Jul. 1907.
    1. "Mandoline"

Trans. by Arthur Symons.
Pencil holograph of no. 1 in MH-H.

W137. Three Songs, 1908.
    1. "Bring Her Again, oh Wester Wind"
    2. "The Nightengale has a Lyre of Gold" (composed
       Feb. 1908)
    3. "The Sea is Full of Wandering Foam"

Texts by W. E. Henley.
Pencil holograph of no. 2 and ink holograph of no. 1-3
in MH-H.

W138. "The Garden of Shadow," Mar. 1908.

Text by Ernest Dowson.
Ink holograph in MH-H.

W139. "Verirrte Reiter," Jan. 1910.

Text by Martin Arudt.
Two ink holographs in MH-H.

W140. "When I am Dead my Dearest," Nov. 1910 (rev. Jan.
1911).

Text by Christina Rosetti.
Ink holograph in MH-H.

W141. "A Song to the Lute," Oct. 1913.

Text by Austin Dobson.
Two ink holographs in MH-H.

W142. <u>Three Songs Without Text</u>, 1939.

Arranged for orchestra, W42.

Premiere:
W142a. 10 May 1940, All-Hill Concert in honor of his
retirement, Paine Hall, Harvard University, Doris
Doe, voice; Jesús Mariá Sanromá, piano.

W143. "By Loe Pool," n.d. (left unfinished).

Text by Arthur Symons.
Ink holograph in MH-H.

W144. "The Land of Love," n.d.

Text by Henry Copley Greene.
Ink holograph in MH-H.

W145. "Oh Roses for the Flush of Youth," n.d.

Text by Christina Rossetti.
Pencil holograph in MH-H.

W146. "Seal Lullaby," n.d.

> Text by Rudyard Kipling.
> Two pencil holographs in MH-H.

W147. <u>Seven Wind Songs</u>, n.d.
>   1. "Wind of the Northern Land"
>   2. "Wind of the Low Red North"
>   3. "Wind of the April Stars"
>   4. "Wind of the Summer Morn"
>   5. "Wind of the Gulfs of Night"
>   6. "Wind of the Outer Waste"
>   7. "Wind of the Driven Snow"

> Texts by Bliss Carman.
> Pencil holograph of no. 1 and ink holographs of nos.
> 1-7 in MH-H.

W148. "Silver and Blue" from <u>Monduock Invaded</u>, n.d.

> Text by Henry Copley Greene.
> Two ink holographs (one left unfinished) in MH-H.

W149. "They are not Long the Weeping and the Laughter," n.d.

> Text by Ernest Dowson.
> Ink holograph in MH-H.

W150. "The Waters are Rising and Flowing," n.d.

> Text by George MacDonald.
> Ink holograph in MH-H.

W151. "When Birds are Songless," n.d.

> Text by William Watson.
> Two ink holographs in MH-H.

<u>Music for Solo Voice and Piano Duet</u>

W152. Arrangement of <u>Autumn Twilight</u> for voice and one
>   piano, four hands, n.d.

> Arrangement of W41.
> Copyist's manuscript in MH-H.

Miscellaneous

W153. <u>Piece for Flute</u>, Jul. 1942.

Ink holograph in OCU.

W154. <u>Piece for Harmonium</u>, n.d.

Dedication: "For H[enry] B[arker or Bixby] H[ill]"
Pencil sketch in MH-H.

W155. [Pieces for Organ,] I and II, n.d.

Pencil sketch of I and II in MH-H.

Bibliography
of Writings
by Hill

This annotated bibliography presents works written by
Edward Burlingame Hill himself (denoted with identifiers
beginning with "H"). There are three sections in this
chapter: 1) book and articles; 2) reviews from Hill's
years as critic for the Boston Evening Transcript; and 3)
program notes written by Hill. Citations here are cross-
referenced with appropriate entries in the "Works and
Performances" ("W") and "Discography" ("D") chapters: for
example, "See W125" refers the reader to the "Works and
Performances" chapter, item 125.

Book and Articles

H1.   "Alexander Glazunoff." Etude 23 (1905), 53.

       Hill provides a brief biography of the Russian
       composer and a description of his pieces.

H2.   "Arthur Foote." Etude 25 (1907), 441.

       Hill offers a short biography of Foote and a survey
       of his works. "Doubtless his most individual works
       are the chamber music, especially the quartet and
       quintet, which must rank among the best products of
       the American composers in their field."

H3.   Associate editor of The Art of Music: A Comprehensive
       Library of Information for Music Lovers and Musi-
       cians. Editor-in-chief Daniel Gregory Mason. Asso-

ciate editors E. B. Hill and Leland Hall. 14 vols.
New York: National Society of Music, 1915-17.

Hill edited vol. 3, _Modern Music_, with Ernest Newman
and contributed the Introduction, Ch. 9 ("The
Followers of César Franck"), and Ch. 10 ("Debussy
and the Ultra-Modernists") to it, pp. 3:vii-xxii,
3:277-316, 3:317-365. These chapters provide a
survey of late nineteenth- and early twentieth-
century French music.

H4.   Autobiographical sketch in Ewen, David. _Composers of_
Today: A Comprehensive Biographical and Critical
Guide to Modern Composers of All Nations. New York:
H. W. Wilson, 1934.

Ewen prints in full on pp. 112-113 an
autobiographical sketch written by Hill.

H5.   "The Bugbear of Method." _Etude_ 20 (1902), 12.

Hill disparages the notion of a pedagogical "method"
in teaching piano students. He recommends that
students choose a teacher not because of the
purported "method" he or she espouses, but one "who
sees definitely the proper relations between
technic, interpretation, and individuality."

H6.   "Business System and Practice." _Musician_ 9 (1904),
344.

In comparing piano lessons with a business, Hill
advocates that a students and teacher plan a careful
system of learning and practice.

H7.   "The Call of the Future." _Musician_ 9 (1904), 376-377.

Hill encourages students to strive for goals, to
think of the future, as they work day to day.

H8.   "Charles Martin Loeffler." _Modern Music_ 13 (1935-36),
26-31.

Hill voices unqualified respect for Loeffler as a
musician and a composer. He presents a short
biography and brief descriptions of Loeffler's
major works. He traces the composer's musical
idiom to his Parisian years--to Bizet, Lalo,
Chabrier, Fauré, and Debussy. Yet he recognizes
that Loeffler "attained his own style and delivered
his personal message" (p. 31). Hill asserts that
Loeffler "has done more than produce works of
impeccable craftsmanship and creative originality
that are without equal among American composers. He
has contributed significantly to the musical
literature of the world" (p. 31).

H9.   "Christian Sinding." _Etude_ 23 (1905), 314.

Hill provides a brief biography of the Norwegian composer and pianist and offers a short assessment of his works.

H10. "Chorus Conducting and Music Festival Organization." Etude 24 (1906), 285-286.

This article prints an interview Hill conducted with Emil Mollenhauer and George Stewart about arranging and carrying out music festivals.

H11. "Claude Debussy's Piano Music." Musician 11 (1906), 375-376.

Hill provides a quick sketch of Debussy's piano music for piano teachers and students.

H12. "Copland's Jazz Concerto in Boston." Modern Music 4/4 (May-Jun. 1927), 35-37.

Hill reports on the controversial nature of this performance and Koussevitzky's courage in performing it. He comments on the "formal balance, fertility of resource and economy in development" (p. 36). Concerning the "dissonant idiom" of the work, Hill notes that Copland "may have overdone matters," but that "without abating one whit of his harmonic acidity, Copland may convert us to his viewpoint" (p. 37). Hill admires "the truly alchemic manner in which Copland has transmuted the dross of jazz into a fantastic and scintillant symphonic style. In this respect he has far transcended all previous similar essays known to the writer" (p. 37).

H13. "A Course in Listening for Piano Students," I-IV. Musician 11 (1906), 281, 343, 429, 537.

Hill offers guidelines for developing a keener ear in rhythm, melody, harmony, and form.

H14. "Debussy's 'Pelléas et Mélisande.'" Musician 13 (1908), 211-240.

Hill summarizes for music teachers and students the plot of the opera and the salient musical features.

H15. "The Development of Programme Music." Music 20 (1901), 26-31, 76-84, 161-166, 225-229, 391-395.

Based on Hill's senior thesis at Harvard, this series of articles traces descriptive music from bird imitations in sixteenth-century songs to the symphonic poems of Richard Strauss and the leitmotif system of Wagner. No mention is made of French music after Berlioz or American music, except for a short paragraph on MacDowell.

H16. "Discouragement and Its Remedy." _Musician_ 10 (1905),
      63.

      Hill suggests ways for students to overcome
      discouragement with music lessons.

H17. "A Famous Italian Pupil of Franz Liszt." _Etude_ 25
      (1907), 714.

      Hill provides a short biography of Giovanni Sgambati
      and a brief assessment of his works.

H18. "A Few Hints on Technic." _Etude_ 19 (1901), 353.

      Hill discusses two hints of on technique: "Do not
      forget to give the fourth and fifth fingers _in both
      hands_ free play"; and "Do not be afraid to reach in
      for black keys, even in passages to be played
      otherwise with a quiet hand."

H19. "Frederick S. Converse." _Musician_ 14 (1909), 164-165.

      Hill presents a brief biography of Converse and a
      survey of his works up to Op. 26. He praises
      Converse for his "long and patient schooling with
      Paine, Chadwick, and Rheinberger; the gradual
      mastery of the resources of academic form; . . . the
      series of symphonic poems; . . . [and] the
      introduction of the dramatic element . . . in which
      the technic of form and orchestra must be at one's
      finger-tips in order to express the emotion of the
      drama" (p. 165).

H20. "The Future of Music at Harvard." _Harvard Graduates'
      Magazine_ 15 (1906-07), 388-391.

      Not yet a professor at Harvard, Hill makes a plea
      for increased support of the Music Department
      there. He points out "the necessity of a more
      adequate provision for the interests of collegiate
      education in music. It is only on the assumption of
      a survival of the profound Puritan distrust for
      aesthetic sensations that one can explain the
      difficulties that have confronted the entry of the
      Fine Arts into the curriculum of a liberal
      education" (p. 389).

H21. "Gabriel Fauré's Piano Music. _Musician_ 16 (1911),
      511, 561.

      Hill divides Fauré's piano music into three groups:
      "the early experimental stage; the spontaneous,
      ebullient period; the later, mature style with a
      somewhat involved harmonic and melodic treatment"
      (p. 511). After noting the admirable quality of the
      pieces in general, he notes: "Although his melody
      at times smacks too much of the salon, its essential

purity and subtle charm cause one to overlook its
setting" (pp. 511, 561).

H22.   "Good Investments." Musician 10 (1905), 18.

Hill suggests that students consider their talent as
a property held in trust and attempt to "make good"
on this investment.

H23.   "Gustave Charpentier." Musician 10 (1905), 318-319.

Hill provides a biographical sketch of Charpentier
and a short summary and critique of his works.

H24.   "Gustave Mahler." Musician 16 (1911), 443.

Hill laments that the managers of the Philharmonic
Orchestra in New York "harassed [Mahler] into
illness, from which he had not the recuperative
power to rally. Such is the responsibility which
rests upon the careless superficiality of officials
in the Philharmonic Society." Of the music, Hill
claims that "it seems just to say that the time is
not ripe for an adequate discussion of his works. .
. . When the shock of their extreme novelty of style
has worn off, one can then judge more accurately of
their intrinsic merit."

H25.   "The Harmonic Dilemma." Musician 16 (1911), 585.

Hill attempts to pinpoint the quandary facing young
composers. Perhaps in testimony to his own dilemma,
he writes, "On one hand, he has painfully acquired
an acquaintance with severe and formal rules, which
. . . demand due recognition of underlying
principles. On the other, he cannot but observe
that the practice of modern composers not only
markedly conflicts with theory, but in many cases
seems to ignore it altogether." He recommends that
a student learn classic harmony, then "he can trust
himself to express his inner convictions with
spontaneity."

H26.   "Harvard Men in Music." Boston Evening Transcript, 22
May 1908, 3:4.

Hill covers the contributions of Harvard graduates
to the musical life of the United States. He pays
particular attention to Arthur Foote, Frederick S.
Converse, and Percy L. Atherton. He also notes
those who have become teachers and critics.

H27.   "The Height of the Piano Chair." Etude 19 (1901),
141.

Hill discusses the three most common heights of the
piano chair in relation to the piano. He advocates

the more traditional one (with elbows slightly below
the level of the keyboard."

H28.   "Hidden Strength." _Musician_ 10 (1905), 232-233.

Hill sets up Vladimir de Pachmann as an example of
someone who drew on hidden strength against all odds
to become a successful musician.

H29.   "Hints on System for Music Teachers." _Etude_ 22
(1904), 397.

Hill advocates setting up clear goals, defining a
plan for each student's practice time, compiling a
record of each pupil's course of study, and in
general pursuing "a more rational and systematic
exercise of [the teacher's] duties."

H30.   "How much shall I correct my Pupils?" _Etude_ 22
(1904), 236.

Hill recommends that teachers correct and criticize
a pupil depending on the student's natural ability
and his or her reaction to correction.

H31.   "How to Interest Students in Technic." _Etude_ 21
(1903), 340.

Hill recommends that teachers advise piano students
to build strength through calisthenics. Then the
teacher should develop his or her own "muscle-
training at the keyboard."

H32.   "The Importance of Finger Training." _Etude_ 25 (1907),
373.

Hill emphasizes that even "in this hasty and
strenuous age," attention must still be paid to
finger training for piano students.

H33.   "Jazz." _Harvard Graduates' Magazine_ 34 (1925-26),
362-365.

Hill presents "the case for and against jazz" (p.
362) in this very early article on jazz and defends
musicians who use it in their works. "The most
serious obstacles in the way of the use of jazz in
the main movements of symphonic works lie in the
monotony and persistence of its rhythms" (p. 363).
He commends John Alden Carpenter for his use of jazz
idioms in _Concertino_ and _Krazy Kat_. He also praises
George Gershwin: "His musical comedy jazz is
unsurpassable. . . . The 'Rhapsody in Blue' was an
astonishing piece for a novice in this field. That
he is uneasy in a piece of this length is obvious,
but despite its defects it is better than the
illusory jazz of some 'high-brow' composers" (p.
365).

H34.   "Josef Hofmann." _Musician_ 12 (1907), 133.

Hill provides a biographical sketch of Hofmann and an assessment of his career and works.

H35.   "Lessons from the Piano Player." _Etude_ 22 (1904), 315.

Hill discusses what a mechanical player piano can teach students. He highlights the "marvelous evenness and distinctness of technique;" the more economical use of accents; the limitations of playing slow pieces like a player piano; the helplessness of a player piano to achieve a varied tone; and the difference that good use of the pedals makes.

H36.   "MacDowell's Marionettes." _Musician_ 15 (1910), 653, 703.

Hill compares the two versions of MacDowell's _Marionettes_, Op. 38. He claims that the composer had "the view of simplifying the unnecessary technical demands and giving more unity to the group" (p. 653). He then cites specific passages that have been revised.

H37.   "The Making of a Russian Pianist: Josef Lhévinne." _Etude_ 24 (1906), 627.

Hill conducted an interview with Lhévinne and prints much of it here. A large portion has to do with the Moscow Conservatory.

H38.   "Maurice Ravel." _Musical Quarterly_ 13 (1927), 130-146.

Hill offers a brief biography and a survey of Ravel's works. Of Ravel's place in modern French music, Hill writes, "If he cannot assume the place of a pioneer, he may at least claim the rewards of legitimate expansion of method. The classic leanings in his style maintain his affinity with the past, yet he is both emphatically of his period, and still capable of absorbing and reproducing the best in the spirit of the present" (p. 146).

H39.   "Maurice Ravel's Piano Music." _Musician_ 12 (1907), 281-282.

Hill provides for piano teachers and students a quick sketch of Ravel's piano works.

H40.   "Method and Individuality." _Musician_ 10 (1905), 102.

Hill notes that there must be a balance between method and individuality. The student must submit to his or her teacher's method, and the teacher must allow the student to grow in an individual way.

H41. Modern French Music. Cambridge, Mass.: Houghton Mifflin Co., 1924. Reprint ed., New York: Da Capo Press, 1969.

In this work, his only book, Hill traces modern French music from the Franco-Prussian War to the early 1920s. He first explores the rise of instrumental music and the decline of opera in late nineteenth-century France. He then describes the beginnings of modernism, claiming that Emmanuel Chabrier was "the unquestioned pioneer of the progressive type of French music" (p. 60). Chapters on Fauré, d'Indy, Debussy, and Ravel follow, with other composers treated in groups in chapters entitled "The Heritage of Franck," "Some Modernist Types," "Figures of the Present," and "A Group of Iconoclasts." Hill claims that "the 'Groupe des Six' are eminently French in their environment, but in their general technical procedures they are as subservient to Stravinsky and Schönberg as their aesthetic forbears of a generation or so ago were to Wagner" (p. 384).

H42. "Modern Technic and Modern Education." Etude 21 (1903), 93.

Hill discusses recent developments in piano technique. He admonishes teachers to continue in the "severe, practical, elementary training" before letting students experiment.

H43. "Muscle vs. Mind." Musician 10 (1905), 152.

Hill notes that the muscular system and the mind must work together in order for the piano student to gain a good technique.

H44. "Music and Health." Musician 9 (1904), 465, 472.

Hill makes a connection between successful piano study and good health and encourages students to exercise, eat well, and get enough sleep.

H45. "Music Lessons by the Great Masters," I-V. Etude 26 (1908), 18, 92-93, 160-161, 222-223, 494-495.

Hill discusses the keyboard teaching techniques of Couperin, Rameau, and C. P. E. Bach; Haydn, Mozart, and Beethoven; Mendelssohn and Schumann; Chopin; and Liszt.

H46. "La musique à Boston." Revue musicale 4/4 (1923), 75-76.

Hill reports on recent performances in Boston, especially of works by French and American composers. He discusses, for example, the Boston Symphony Orchestra's performance of Honegger's <u>Horace Victorieux</u> and Griffes's <u>Clouds</u> and <u>The White Peacock</u>.

H47. "La musique à Boston." <u>Revue musicale</u> 7/6 (1926), 78-79.

Hill touches on the important premieres in Boston, including the Boston Symphony Orchestra's performance of Ibert's <u>Escales</u>, Tansman's <u>Sinfonietta</u>, Satie's <u>Gymnopédies</u>, Loeffler's <u>Memories of my Childhood</u>, Bloch's <u>Suite</u>, and Copland's <u>Music for the Theatre</u>. Of the last he writes, "l'oeuvre est moins intéressante que sa <u>Symphonie</u> pour orgue et orchestre" (p. 79).

H48. "La musique américaine contemporaine." <u>Revue musicale</u> 4/1 (1922), 68-72, and 4/2 (1922), 171-173.

Hill offers a summary of modern American music. He dates the beginning of "notre vie artistique sérieuse" (p. 68) at around 1870. Discussion of the founding of American orchestras, the beginning of music study in the universities, and the problem of native popular music precede an examination of the most prominent American composers. He calls J. K. Paine "le premier compositeur américain qui me paraisse digne d'être pris en considération" (p. 70). He traces the careers of Paine, Chadwick, Kelly, Parker, MacDowell, Loeffler, Converse, Hadley, Gilbert, Mason, and Carpenter.

H49. "La musique aux tats-Unis." <u>Revue musicale</u> 2/3 (1921), 267-268.

Hill reports on recent premieres and developments in the United States. He notes the growing number of orchestras. He praises the <u>Concertino</u> of John Alden Carpenter and the concerts of Eva Gauthier. He also notes the new French and American works played by the Boston Symphony Orchestra under Pierre Monteux during the 1920-21 season.

H50. "Music at Harvard." <u>Boston Evening Transcript</u>, 15 Dec. 1906, 2:8.

Hill presents a short history of the music department of Harvard University.

H51. "A New American Composer: Frederick S. Converse and His Career." <u>Musician</u> 11 (1906), 188-189.

Hill introduces Converse through a short biography and an assessment of his career.

H52.   "Nicolas Rimsky-Korsakoff." _Etude_ 25 (1907), 508.

Hill provides a brief biographical sketch of the
composer and a short assessment of his works.

H53.   "Nicolas Rimsky-Korsakoff." _Musician_ 13 (1908), 396,
423.

This is very similar to the above article.

H54.   "Our Best Efforts and Their Results." _Musician_ 9
(1904), 174.

Hill praises "technique" over "method" and
emphasizes the importance of concentration during
piano practice.

H55.   "The Piano-Player's Position." _Etude_ 20 (1902), 416-
417.

Hill discusses his view of how piano players should
sit at the piano.

H56.   "The Progress of Music at Harvard." _Harvard_
Graduates' Magazine 16 (1907-08), 270-274.

Written almost a year before Hill began teaching at
Harvard, this article describes the strides made by
the Music Department and the continued need to
support it with adequate funds. "For inasmuch as
Harvard College took the pioneer step 30 years ago,
to retract anything of her high attitude in the
past, to hamper the free development of conditions
in the present, and to be blind to the pressing
needs of the future, would be to deny the signal
achievement of those American composers, critics,
and writers on music whose faith and unfaltering
effort have helped to secure esteem and respect for
their country's art" (p. 274).

H57.   "Progress--Past and Present." _Etude_ 25 (1907), 778.

Hill advocates an open attitude towards new music,
even as older music is still enjoyed.

H58.   "Ravel in Retrospect." _Boston Evening Transcript_, 22
Jan. 1938.

Written shortly after the death of Ravel, this
article provides an assessment of his work. Hill
asserts that Ravel "antedated Debussy in the use of
the pentatonic scale" and that "he was the first in
the 'Habanera' (1895) to use a Spanish idiom, and to
set verses by an old French poet, Clement Marot, in
the 'Epigrammes.'" He admits that "Ravel cannot
take rank as a composer of songs with Faure, Duparc
and Debussy."

H59. "Reality and Poetry." _Musician_ 10 (1905), 190-191.

Hill encourages students to balance reality and
imagination in their interpretations of music.

H60. "A Review of Music During 1907." _Musician_ 13 (1908),
18-19.

Hill notes the premieres, important musical events,
and deaths that took place in 1907. "Probably the
most significant achievement in new productions of
the year was that on November 22 and 23 by the
Boston Symphony Orchestra, of Mr. Charles Martin
Loeffler's _Pagan Poem_."

H61. "Richard Strauss' 'Salome.'" _Musician_ 12 (1907), 30-
31.

Hill provides an introduction for music teachers and
students of Strauss's work.

H62. "The Rise of Modern French Music." _Etude_ 32 (1914),
253-254.

Hill contributes a short introduction to the major
figures of modern French music. He highlights the
careers of Chabrier, Fauré, Franck, d'Indy,
Chausson, Bruneau, Charpentier, Debussy, Ravel, and
Dukas.

H63. "The Secret of Success." _Musician_ 9 (1904), 425.

Hill discusses two keys to success for piano
students, "talent and power to work."

H64. "The Secret of Successful Work." _Etude_ 24 (1906),
110.

Hill offers advice to teachers on how to encourage
music students to practice and succeed in their
lessons.

H65. "Self-Reliance or Dependence." _Musician_ 9 (1904),
344.

Hill praises those self-reliant students who
motivate themselves to achieve excellence.

H66. "Sergei Rachmaninoff." _Etude_ 23 (1905), 185.

Hill provides a brief biography of Rachmaninoff and
a critical assessment of his works.

H67. "Significant Phases of Modern French Music." _Etude_ 32
(1914), 489-490.

In this sequel to "The Rise of Modern French Music,"
Hill provides short excerpts from the music of

several French composers and explains the major technical advances.

H68.   "La situation musicale aux tats-Unis et son influence sur les créateurs." <u>Revue musicale</u> 2/6 (1921), 78-79.

Hill points up several symptoms of an unhealthy environment for American composers. These include the "prima donna" attitude of conductors and performers; the dependence on older, more traditional works in the repertories of symphony orchestras; the sometimes artificial search for a native music; and audiences' desire to hear grand, romantic works.

H69.   "The Study of the Pupil." <u>Etude</u> 22 (1904), 12.

Hill admonishes piano teachers to augment their expertise on methods and technique with an understanding of each student in his or her individuality.

H70.   "Superfluous Technique." <u>Musician</u> 9 (1904), 218.

Hill argues that while "it is indeed true that this is an age of technique, and that there are many pianists appearing in public who are content to display technique and nothing else, . . . it would be difficult to argue . . . against the acquisition of technique."

H71.   "Synopsis of Modern French Music." <u>Musician</u> 17 (1912), 593, 666, 712, 742-743, 784; 18 (1913), 134-135, 350-351, 422-423.

Hill presents a six-part layperson's introduction to the important personalities and compositions of modern French music. He summarizes the contributions of Chabrier, Fauré, d'Indy, Chausson, Duparc, Lekeu, Bruneau, Charpentier, Debussy, Dukas, and Ravel. The essential organization and main arguments are much the same, though not as fully developed, as in his book of twelve years later.

H72.   "Talent vs. Self-Development." <u>Etude</u> 25 (1907), 644.

In assessing piano students' potential, Hill concludes: "With all possible honor for talent in its various manifestations, we must reserve especial appreciation for the faculty of self-development."

H73.   "The Thomas Orchestra: The Impressions of an Eastern Listener." <u>Boston Evening Transcript</u>, 18 Dec. 1907, 25.

Hill evaluates Chicago's Orchestra and its conductor, Frederick Stock. Of the orchestra, he

notes that "in accurate ensemble, in vigor of
attack, in vitality of interpretation, this
orchestra is most exceptional." Of Stock, he points
out that "no progressive movement in modern music
has escaped Mr. Stock's attention. . . . Best of
all, he is ever ready to give an honest hearing of
works by American composers."

H74.   "The Treatment of the Thumb." Etude 20 (1902), 211.

Hill discusses methods of playing with the thumb.
He recognizes that "short-cuts" and new techniques
have to be used in more modern music.

H75.   "The True Basis of Technic." Etude 18 (1900), 401.

Hill emphasizes that in the face of new
"ultramodern" techniques, students and teachers must
be reminded "never [to] overlook the simple facts of
technic,--fingers, wrist, and arms."

H76.   "A True Interpreter of Chopin." Etude 23 (1905), 19.

Hill offers a biographical sketch and critical
assessment of Vladimir de Pachmann, whom Hill
forwards as one of the best interpreters of Chopin.

H77.   "The Uses of Frivolity." Musician 12 (1907), 432-433.

Hill notes the importance of mental diversion for
music students. He cites the leisure activities of
famous musicians.

H78.   "Vacation Plans." Musician 9 (1904), 303.

Hill recommends that music students keep up their
studies in some capacity during their vacations but
also to refresh themselves mentally and physically.

H79.   "The Value of Conservatism." Musician 9 (1904), 267.

Hill encourages students to cultivate a thorough
education in the classical music literature and not
to be lured only by the latest experiments.

H80.   "Vincent d'Indy." Etude 24 (1906), 18.

Hill sketches d'Indy's biography and describes his
works.

H81.   "Vincent d'Indy." Musician 11 (1906), 400-401.

This is almost identical to the above article.

H82.   "Vincent d'Indy à Boston." Revue musicale 2/1 (1921),
       272-273.

Hill reports on d'Indy's visit to Boston and offers
a brief description of the composer's <u>Poème des
Rivages</u> (op. 77). He writes of the work, "La
structure de ces pièces est simple et claire,
cohérente et pleine; le contenu musical se suffit
pleinement à lui-même sans jamais viser à la
description. . . . l'art de Vincent d'Indy a été si
direct, si humain, si éloigné de toute préoccupation
intellectuelle" (p. 273).

H83.   "Vincent d'Indy: An Estimate." <u>Musical Quarterly</u> 1
(1915), 246-259.

Hill offers a thorough examination of d'Indy's life
and works up through 1915. After discussing several
of d'Indy's major works, Hill assesses his
weaknesses and strengths. Among the former he cites
d'Indy's "overbalance in the intellectual aspects of
his art;" "his preoccupation in behalf of the
architectural and stylistic elements" (p. 256); and
"the confluence of interests in d'Indy's own style"
(p. 257). Yet he praises d'Indy because "he has
reaffirmed and reasserted the value and
practicability of using the classic forms, treated
with basic fidelity to their stylistic essence" (p.
258).

H84.   Review of Claire Reis's <u>Composers in America:
Biographical Sketches of Living Composers with a
Record of Their Works</u> (New York: MacMillan, 1938)
in <u>Modern Music</u> 15 (1937-38), 197-198.

Hill offers a favorable review of this volume. Hill
notices in the worklists "a marked increase in
works for chamber music or chamber orchestra, and .
. . stage works, particularly the ballet. . . . It
was a foregone conclusion that the American composer
would continue along the well-trodden paths of
instrumental music, . . . but his awakening to the
call of the ballet is a sign of esthetic
independence to be welcomed with rejoicing" (p.
198).

<u>Reviews for the "Boston Evening Transcript"</u>

H85.   "Arenski's Piano Concerto in Cambridge." <u>BET</u>, 6 May
1907, 13.

The Boston Symphony Orchestra with Olga von Radecki,
piano.

H86.   "Association Hall: Mr. Giguère's Recital." <u>BET</u>, 11
Dec. 1901, 2:17.

Chambord Giguère, violin.

H87. "Association Hall: Mr. Giguère's Recital." <u>BET</u>, 16
Dec. 1901, 4.

Chambord Giguère, violin.

H88. "Carl Baermann Comes out of Retirement." <u>BET</u>, 5 Feb.
1907, 13.

Carl Baermann, piano.

H89. "Chickering Hall: Boston Singing Club." <u>BET</u>, 10 Apr.
1902, 11.

H90. "Chickering Hall: Boston Symphony Quartet." <u>BET</u>, 20
Nov. 1906, 13.

H91. "Chickering Hall: Chamber Concert." <u>BET</u>, 21 Nov.
1906, 17.

Hoffmann Quartet and Félix Fox, piano.

H92. "Chickering Hall: 'Enoch Arden.'" <u>BET</u>, 20 Feb. 1902,
21.

Melodrama by Strauss performed by George Riddle,
reading voice, and B. J. Lang, piano.

H93. "Chickering Hall: Josef Hofmann's Recital." <u>BET</u>, 9
Dec. 1901, 7.

Josef Hofmann, piano.

H94. "Chickering Hall: Miss Clemens and Miss Nichols'
Joint Recital." <u>BET</u>, 27 Nov. 1907, 23.

Clara Clemens, contralto; Marie Nichols, violin.

H95. "Chickering Hall: Miss Sawyer's Recital." <u>BET</u>, 4
Dec. 1901, 15.

Helen Sawyer, piano.

H96. "Chickering Hall: Miss von Radecki's Concert." <u>BET</u>,
20 Apr. 1907, 2:8.

Olga von Radecki, piano.

H97. "Chickering Hall: Mr. Allen's Concert." <u>BET</u>, 3 Apr.
1908, 12.

Paul Hastings Allen, piano; concert of his own
works.

H98. "Chickering Hall: Mr. Copeland's Recital." <u>BET</u>, 23
Apr. 1908, 14.

George Copeland, Jr., piano.

H99. "Chickering Hall: Mr. Dolmetsch's Concert." BET, 14
      Mar. 1907, 13.

Arnold Dolmetsch, director.

H100. "Chickering Hall: Mr. Dolmetsch's Concert." BET, 28
      Mar. 1907, 13.

Arnold Dolmetsch, director.

H101. "Chickering Hall: Mr. Slivinski's Recital." BET, 27
      Nov. 1901, 15.

Joseph Slivinski, piano.

H102. "Chickering Hall: Mrs. Hartmann's Recital." BET, 12
      Apr. 1902, 26.

Florence Hartmann, voice.

H103. "Chickering Hall: St. Luke's Organ Fund Concert."
      BET, 13 Nov. 1901, 21.

H104. "Chickering Hall: T. Adamowski Trio." BET, 4 Apr.
      1902, 11.

H105. "Chickering Hall: The Boston Singing Club." BET, 23
      Jan. 1902, 11.

H106. "Chickering Hall: The Dolmetsch Concert." BET, 27
      Feb. 1908, 12.

Arnold Dolmetsch, director.

H107. "Chickering Hall: The Kneisel Quartet." BET, 11 Mar.
      1902, 12.

H108. "Chickering Hall: The Kneisel Quartet." BET, 16 Jan.
      1907, 17.

H109. "Chickering Hall: The Symphony Quartet." BET, 23
      Apr. 1907, 14.

H110. "Columbia Theatre: 'The Mikado.'" BET, 19 Nov. 1901,
      12.

Grand Opera Company.

H111. "The Concerts of Yesterday." BET, 14 Dec. 1906, 13.

H112. "The Concerts of Yesterday." BET, 18 Dec. 1906, 14.

The Boston Symphony Quartet and Otto Neitzel, piano.

H113. "Dr. Muck Plays Brockway's Youthful Symphony." BET, 6
      Apr. 1903, 2:6.

H114. "Edgar Tinel and his Three 'Tone-Pictures.'" BET, 7
      Feb. 1907, 11.

H115. "Faneuil Hall: Verdi Concert." BET, 28 Feb. 1902,
      11.

H116. "Huntington Chambers Hall: Miss Heinrich." BET, 21
      Mar. 1902, 9.

      Julia Heinrich, voice.

H117. "Huntington Chambers Hall: Mrs. Guckenberg's
      Recital." BET, 31 Jan. 1902, 11

      Margaret Guckenberg, mezzo-contralto.

H118. "Jordan Hall: Miss Goodson's Recital." BET, 15 Mar.
      1907, 13.

      Katharine Goodson, piano.

H119. "Jordan Hall: Mr. Anthony's Recital." BET, 26 Nov.
      1907, 14.

      Charles Anthony, piano.

H120. "Jordan Hall: Mr. Debuchy's Concert." BET, 29 Oct.
      1907, 14.

      Albert Debuchy, voice.

H121. "Jordan Hall: Mr. Tew's Recital." BET, 10 Jan. 1907.

      Whitney Tew, bass.

H122. "Jordan Hall: Mrs. Hall's Concert." BET, 22 Jan.
      1908, 12.

      Mrs. Richard J. Hall, organizer; George Longy,
      conductor.

H123. "Jordan Hall: The Apollo Club." BET, 22 Nov. 1906,
      13.

H124. "Jordan Hall: The Apollo Club." BET, 21 Nov. 1907,
      14.

H125. "Jordan Hall: The Boston Singing Club." BET, 12 Mar.
      1908, 13.

H126. "Kreisler's Last Recital for the Present." BET, 3
      Feb. 1908, 13.

      Fritz Kreisler, violin.

H127. "Louis Bachner Reappears." BET, 24 Jan. 1908, 12.

Louis Bachner, piano.

H128. "Miss Terry's Concert." BET, 4 Feb. 1908, 13.

Fay Cord, soprano; Francis Rogers, baritone; Jessie
Davis, piano.

H129. "Mme. Gadski Reappears." BET, 1 Feb. 1908, 2:6.

Johanna Gadski, voice.

H130. "Mr. Converse's 'Job': An Outline of his Newest
Composition." BET, 28 Sep. 1907, 2:6.

H131. "Mr. De Gogorza's Concert." BET, 17 Mar. 1908, 14.

Emilio de Gogorza, voice.

H132. "Mr. Dolmetsch Resumes his Concerts." BET, 28 Dec.
1907, 3:4.

Arnold Dolmetsch, director.

H133. "Mr. Gebhard and the Longy Club at Milton." BET, 17
Apr. 1908, 13.

Heinrich Gebhard, piano.

H134. "Mr. Maurel Reappears at a Song Recital." BET, 5 Dec.
1907, 14.

Victor Maurel, voice.

H135. "The Pierian Concert." BET, 22 May 1908, 3:4.

Pierian Sodality of Harvard University.

H136. "The Pierian Sodality Musically." BET, 13 Apr. 1908,
13.

Pierian Sodality of Harvard University.

H137. "Potter Hall: Miss Fletcher's Recital." BET, 6 Dec.
1906, 13.

Nina Fletcher, violin.

H138. "Potter Hall: The Hoffmann Quartet." BET, 6 Mar.
1907, 17.

H139. "Potter Hall: The Longy Club." BET, 11 Feb. 1908,
13.

H140. "Professor Paine's Opera. His 'Azara' to be Heard at
Last." BET, 6 Apr. 1907, 2:6.

H141. "A Recital by Miss Wood and Miss Collier." BET, 13
Feb. 1908, 12.

Anna Miller Wood, mezzo-contralto; Bessie Bell
Collier, violin; Malcolm Lang, piano.

H142. "Sanders Theatre: The Pierian Concert." BET, 4 Dec.
1901, 15.

Pierian Sodality of Harvard University.

H143. "Steinert Hall: Mr. Bendix's Recital." BET, 3 Dec.
1901, 2:5.

Max Bendix, violin.

H144. "Steinert Hall: Mr. Copeland's Recital." BET, 28
Feb. 1908, 12.

George Copeland, Jr., piano.

H145. "Steinert Hall: Mr. Denghausen's Recital." BET, 16
Nov. 1907, 3:6.

A. F. Denghausen, voice.

H146. "Steinert Hall: Mr. Fox's Concert." BET, 7 Mar.
1907, 13.

Félix Fox, piano.

H147. "Steinert Hall: Mr. Fox's Recital." BET, 4 Jan.
1907, 12.

Félix Fox, piano.

H148. "Steinert Hall: Mr. Hall's Recital." BET, 30 Oct.
1907, 17.

Leland Hall, piano.

H149. "Steinert Hall: Mr. Hall's Recital." BET, 7 Nov.
1907, 12.

Leland Hall, piano.

H150. "Steinert Hall: Mr. Klahre's Recital." BET, 10 Dec.
1901, 9.

Edwin Klahre, piano.

H151. "Steinert Hall: Mr. Klahre's Recital." BET, 7 Feb.
1902, 9.

Edwin Klahre, piano.

H152. "Steinert Hall: Slivinski's Recital." BET, 27 Feb.
1902, 11.

Joseph Slivinski, piano.

H153. "Steinert Hall: The Adamowski Trio." BET, 24 Feb.
        1908, 13.

H154. "Steinert Hall: The Belcher Quartet." BET, 6 Mar.
        1908, 12.

H155. "The Symphony Concert." BET, 19 Jan. 1907, 3:4.

H156. "The Symphony Concert." BET, 30 Dec. 1907, 9.

H157. "The Symphony Concert." BET, 18 Jan. 1908, 2:6.

H158. "The Symphony Concert." BET, 25 Jan. 1908, 3:4.

H159. "The Symphony Concert: Mr. Muck's Programme of
        Romantic Music." BET, 14 Dec. 1907, 2:6.

H160. "Symphony Hall: Dubois's Cantata." BET, 3 Feb. 1902,
        11.

H161. "Symphony Hall: 'Elijah.'" BET, 12 Nov. 1901, 11.

        The Handel and Haydn Society.

H162. "Symphony Hall: Mr. Lemare's Recital." BET, 3 Apr.
        1902, 11.

        Edwin H. Lemare, organ.

H163. "Symphony Hall: Sousa's Band." BET, 20 Jan. 1902,
        11.

H164. "Symphony Hall: Symphony Concert." BET, 17 Mar.
        1902, 11.

H165. "Symphony Hall: 'The Messiah.'" BET, 26 Dec. 1901,
        10.

        The Handel and Haydn Society.

H166. "Tremont Temple: Municipal Concert." BET, 17 Dec.
        1901, 12.

        Emil Mollenhauer, conductor.

H167. "A Visiting Orchestra." BET, 19 Feb. 1907, 14.

        Pittsburgh Orchestra, Emil Paur, conductor.

Program Notes

H168. "Concertino for Piano and Orchestra, Op. 36." Boston

Symphony Orchestra Program, 25 April 1932, 1931-32
season, 12-14.

"Although in one movement, there are the usual three
sections of a concerto. . . . There is a family
resemblance between the themes of the different
sections, but there can scarcely be said to be a
'cyclical method' as applied by Franck and his
pupils" (p. 12).

H169. "The Fall of the House of Usher, Op. 27." Boston
Symphony Orchestra Program, 29 October 1920, 1920-21
season, 208-212.

"It was not my intention to depict the story scene
by scene but rather to attempt to give in music an
impression of the atmosphere of the story as a
whole. For musical treatment I did associate the
two themes with Roderick and Madeline Usher, but
entirely without descriptive realism save possibly
in the destruction of the house. Structurally the
piece approaches closely the abridged sonata form"
(p. 208).

H170. "Lilacs, Poem for Orchestra, Op. 33." Boston Symphony
Orchestra Program, 31 March 1927, 1926-27 season,
1688.

"Long an admirer of Miss Lowell's poetry, it one day
struck me forcibly that 'Lilacs' was an excellent
'subject' for musical treatment by one of New
England ancestry. On reflection, I soon saw the
impracticability of attempting to follow the poem in
detail, and the present work is the result of
impressions connected with portions of the poem,
chiefly the beginning and the end" (p. 1688).

H171. "Music for English Horn and Orchestra, Op. 50."
Boston Symphony Orchestra Program, 2 March 1945,
1944-45 season, 1052-1054.

"The expressive personalities of wind instruments
have always held a peculiar appeal to me. Hence I
have composed sonatas for flute and piano, clarinet
and piano, two sonatas for two unaccompanied
clarinets, as well as a sextet for wind instruments
and piano" (p. 1052).

H172. "Nine Waltzes for Orchestra, Op. 28." Boston
Symphony Orchestra Program, 24 February 1922, 1921-
22 season, 998.

"My waltzes . . . were composed for the piano in the
summer of 1920. Since some of them seemed to
suggest the orchestra, I arranged them all for
orchestra in the autumn and winter of 1920-21. . . .
The last waltz, having an introduction derived from
that preceding, returns to the material of number

one, with slight changes of tonality, with the
object of unifying the set" (p. 998).

H173. "Ode for Mixed Chorus and Orchestra." Boston Symphony
Orchestra Program, 17 October 1930, 1930-31 season,
113-115.

"In the first and last stanzas of the Ode, I have
used a mixed chorus. In the second verse, perhaps
suggested by its sentiment, women's voices alone are
employed. Similarly, for the third verse men's
voices seemed appropriate" (p. 114).

H174. "The Parting of Lancelot and Guinevere, Op. 22."
Boston Symphony Orchestra Program, 24 March 1916,
1915-16 season, 1113-1116.

"After a short introduction, the theme of Guinevere
is heard in the English horn. This is developed
with more and more animation up to the entrance of
Lancelot's theme in the trumpets. This in turn
leads to an episode, based on Guinevere's theme, but
reharmonized and extended, serving as Lancelot's
retrospect upon the love-scene. . . . Then follows
the dramatic conflict of parting, which attains a
climax of some proportions. . . In the last section
a new melody appears in the clarinets over a triplet
figure in the 'cellos and violas, serving as the
basis of a musical epilogue" (p. 1114).

H175. "Scherzo for Two Pianos and Orchestra." Boston
Symphony Orchestra Program, 19 December 1924, 1924-
25 season, 730-732).

"While I am not of those ardent enthusiasts who
affirm that the future of American music lies in a
wholesale assimilation of the 'jazz' style, I
nevertheless sincerely admire its best traits. It
furthermore seems a fitting, if somewhat limited,
field of experiment for the American composer of
serious aims. This problem has already tempted
Messrs. Powell, Carpenter, and Gershwin" (p. 730).

H176. "Sinfonietta in One Movement for Orchestra, Op. 37."
Boston Symphony Orchestra Program, 9 March 1933,
1932-33 season, 826-827.

"Last spring, Dr. Koussevitzky suggested my writing
a symphony in one movement. The resulting material
seemed to approach a sinfonietta rather than a
symphony" (p. 826).

H177. "Stevensoniana Suite No. 2, Op. 29." Boston Symphony
Orchestra Program, 21 March 1924, 1923-24 season,
1364-1372.

"These little pieces, although attempting to reflect

the mood of Stevenson's verses, are not primarily
descriptive music" (p. 1366).

H178. "Symphony in B-flat Major, Op. 34." Boston Symphony
Orchestra Program, 30 March 1928, 1927-28 season,
1663-1664.

"This symphony . . . has no descriptive basis, hints
at no dramatic conflict or spiritual crisis. It
attempts merely to develop musical ideas" (p. 1663).

H179. "Symphony No. 2, Op. 35." Boston Symphony Orchestra
Program, 27 February 1931, 1930-31 season, 1152-
1154.

"This second symphony, like the first, has no
descriptive background, no literary quotations
appended. I find myself in sympathy with those of
the younger generation who feel that music has
enough intrinsic problems of its own without adding
those of other arts. Also, I have kept to the
traditional forms, thinking I had not had sufficient
experience to experiment" (p. 1152).

H180. "Symphony No. 3, Op. 41." Boston Symphony Orchestra
Program, 3 December 1937, 1937-38 season, 350-352.

"It has no descriptive background, and aims merely
to present and develop musical ideas according to
the traditional forms" (p. 350).

Bibliography
of Writings
about Hill

This annotated bibliography presents books and articles
containing passages about Edward Burlingame Hill as well as
reviews of his book and compositions. Each entry is
preceded with an identifier beginning with "B". Citations
here are cross-referenced with appropriate entries in the
"Works and Performances" ("W") and "Discography" ("D")
chapters: for example, "See W75" refers the reader to the
"Works and Performances" chapter, item 75.

Books and Articles

B1.   Ballantine, Edward. "Artist and Teacher." Boston
       Evening Transcript, 23 May 1940, 4:5.

       Ballantine offers a sketch of Hill's life and career
       on the occasion of his retirement from Harvard. Of
       Hill's teaching, Ballantine notes that "he has
       always been patient and generous in giving time to
       students in private conference and to any young
       composer seeking advice." In addition, "he was one
       of the first Americans to appreciate the
       extraordinary musicianship of Nadia Boulanger and
       through his influence a number of his students went
       to Paris to study composition with her."

B2.   Copland, Aaron. The New Music: 1900-1960. Rev. and
       enlarged ed. New York: Norton, 1968.

       Copland includes Hill--along with Carpenter,
       Gruenberg, Piston, McBride, and Gould--in a group of
       composers who "used jazz with greater or lesser
       degrees of politeness" (p. 69).

B3.   Dupree, Mary Herron. "'Jazz,' the Critics, and
       American Art Music in the 1920s." _American Music_ 4
       (1986), 287-301.

       Dupree mentions Hill as an early advocate of jazz
       among "serious" composers. She cites his lecture on
       "Jazz and the Music of Today," given on 10 February
       1924 to the League of Composers, as an important
       early step in boosting its acceptance (p. 289).

B4.   _Harvard College Class of 1894, Fiftieth Anniversary_
       Report, 1894-1944. Norwood, Mass.: Plimpton Press,
       1944.

       This report contains a two-page biography of Hill on
       pp. 256-257.

B5.   Howard, John Tasker. _Our American Music: Three_
       Hundred Years of It. 3rd ed. New York:
       Thomas Y. Crowell Co., 1954.

       Howard presents a biographical sketch of Hill on pp.
       384-386. Of _Stevensoniana_, he notes that "the
       scoring is rich and colorful, with a leaning toward
       the French impressionists; but also with a
       tenderness and simplicity that is altogether
       personal" (p. 384). The _Sinfonietta for String_
       Orchestra "is conservative without suggesting a
       conscious harking back to the past. It has
       individuality and the personal quality Hill aims to
       achieve, as well as lyric charm" (pp. 385-386).

B6.   Howard, John Tasker. _Our Contemporary Composers:_
       American Music in the Twentieth Century. New York:
       Thomas Y. Crowell, 1942.

       Howard offers a biographical sketch and critical
       evaluation of Hill's music on pp. 56-59. "If
       concert-goers expect a university professor to be
       academic in his own music, they are happily
       disappointed in Hill, for whatever they may possess,
       his works certainly lack a pedagogic flavor." "He
       is perfectly willing to risk and admit the
       conservative label, for he frankly confesses his
       inability to write or even think atonally, even
       though he may show an occasional tendency toward
       mild polytonality. He is in thorough sympathy with
       contemporary schools of musical thought, even with
       the radicals, but he realizes that these things are
       not for him as a composer" (p. 57).

B7.   Leichtentritt, Hugo. _Serge Koussevitzky: The Boston_
       Symphony Orchestra and the New American Music.
       Cambridge, Mass.: Harvard University Press, 1946.
       Reprint ed., New York: AMS Press, 1978.

       Leichtentritt discusses the works by Hill that were
       premiered under the baton of Koussevitzky on pp. 31-

36. He praises Hill's "inherent Americanism that contrasts with the noisy, pretentious Americanism in vogue for some time" (p. 31). Of Hill's neo-classic works, he writes, "Refined taste and something serene and amiable gives Hill's later works a unique and distinctive position in recent American music, which generally lacks just these qualities no matter how else it may excel" (p. 33).

B8.   Levy, Alan Howard. Musical Nationalism: American Composers' Search for Identity. Westport: Greenwood Press, 1983.

Levy's first two chapters, "The German Orthodoxy" and "Americanism and French Impressionism" provide an excellent overview of the transition made by American composers from German to French models. He evaluates Hill's contribution to this conversion through his writings and teachings on p. 25.

B9.   Maguire, Helena. "Letters to the Beginning Teacher: The Pantomime, or The True Office of Music: Out of a Talk with Edward B. Hill." Musician 19 (1914), 237.

As she extols the virtues of the pantomime, Maguire notes that "Mr. Hill gives all the credit for the interpretative-ballet to the Russians, yet years ago, when the Russians were only just working out their ideas, and before Mr. Hill had even heard about their new school, . . . he himself wrote and produced a pantomime, Jack Frost in the Summertime, in which he experimented with the very ideas which the Russians have since so successfully developed." Of his newest pantomime, Pan and the Star, she writes, "It is wonderful, beautiful music, and is waiting to be heard; it is the music that America is waiting to hear from her men."

B10.   Mason, Daniel Gregory. "At Harvard in the Nineties." New England Quarterly 9 (1936), 43-70.

Mason describes Hill and musical activities at Harvard on pp. 57-62. Several passages are worth quoting. "Arthur Whiting said of [Hill's] piano-playing that he was 'too much interested in the next note'" (p. 58). "[Hill] was as social in habit as I was solitary; athletics and all forms of sport, so boring to me, filled him with enthusiasm" (p. 58). "Our musical tastes, of course, reflected the general polarity of our temperaments, [Hill] leaning far more than I to the brilliant, the colorful, and the picturesque, and in those college days falling much under the spell of MacDowell, as he later took the French impressionists and the Russian primitivists more seriously than I could" (pp. 59-60).

B11.   Mason, Daniel Gregory. <u>The Dilemma of American Music</u>
       <u>and Other Essays</u>. New York: Macmillan, 1928.

       "Debussy and Ravel are reflected in such
       contemporary American composers as Edward
       Burlingame Hill and John Alden Carpenter. . . .
       Hill, as he has shown in his orchestral suite,
       'Stevensoniana,' can score with a richness and
       clarity of color evidently learned at the feet of
       the French impressionists, though combined with a
       naïveté and tenderness of feeling quite personal.
       In other works, such as 'The Fall of the House of
       Usher,' he is less personal, more conventional, more
       purely reflective" (p. 6).

B12.   Mason, Daniel Gregory. <u>Music in my Time and other</u>
       <u>Reminiscences</u>. New York: MacMillan, 1938.

       The article "At Harvard in the Nineties" is
       reprinted here as Chapters 2 and 3. Hill is
       mentioned throughout the book, and some of their
       correspondence is printed. One letter from Mason to
       Hill confirms the latter's more liberal attitude
       toward modern music. "I have got to a sort of
       transition point in taste . . . a little enamored
       (don't faint) of certain phases of modern style, and
       of course without the technic to satisfy myself in
       any new direction. I hasten to reassure you that my
       'modernism' would not be so considered by you" (p.
       167). Mason also notes a keen observation made by
       Hill about Mason's <u>Quartet on Negro Themes</u> on p.
       366.

B13.   McGlinchee, Claire. "American Literature in American
       Music." <u>Musical Quarterly</u> 31 (1945), 101-119.

       McGlinchee discusses Hill's <u>Fall of the House of</u>
       <u>Usher</u> and <u>Lilacs</u>, among other American works. Of
       the first she writes, "It was the composer's
       intention not to depict the story scene by scene but
       rather to attempt to give an impression through the
       music of the atmosphere of the story as a whole" (p.
       114). About <u>Lilacs</u>, she similarly claims that "Hill
       saw, on reflection, the impracticability of
       attempting to follow the poem in detail. His work
       is the result of impressions connected chiefly with
       the beginning and end of it" (p. 117).

B14.   "Mephisto's Musings." <u>Musical America</u> 40/19 (30 Aug.
       1924), 7.

       The author discusses several anti-jazz campaigns
       being waged across the country. He then writes that
       "Liszt wrote jazz and got away with it. Even a
       Harvard professor of the present time has written
       jazz; and, what's more, he has called it such[,] and
       a more delectable piece of music does not exist than
       this same "Jazz Study" by Edward Burlingame Hill."

B15.   Moore, MacDonald Smith. <u>Yankee Blues: Musical
       Culture and American Identity</u>. Bloomington:
       Indiana University Press, 1985.

       Moore includes Hill in the group of Yankee
       "centennial" composers (i.e., born around 1876) who
       sought to use their music to redeem the American
       spirit. He concentrates on Daniel Gregory Mason and
       Charles Ives as the chief representatives--each in a
       different way--and draws on Hill's career in only a
       few places. Moore fails to mention Hill's more
       liberal attitude toward jazz and toward Jewish
       composers, both of which the majority of
       "centennial" composers opposed. A stimulating study
       of early-twentieth-century American music, this work
       nonetheless fails to note Hill's striking openness
       to musical experimentation.

B16.   Slonimsky, Nicolas. "Composers of New England."
       <u>Modern Music</u> 7/2 (Feb.-Mar. 1930), 24-27.

       "A few American notes [in <u>Lilacs</u>] sound
       unmistakably through an idiom which is otherwise
       international. It is interesting to note that Hill
       is perhaps the only New Englander to intrude on the
       New York field by composing 'serious jazz'" (p. 26).

B17.   Slonimsky, Nicolas. "Tribute to E. B. Hill, Native
       Composer." <u>New York Times</u>, 2 Nov. 1952, X:7.

       This letter to the music editor laments the passing
       of Hill's eightieth birthday without newspaper
       commemorations or orchestral revivals of his works.
       He notes that "at the dawn of this century he was
       the staunch champion of modern French music. . . .
       Historically, he did more than any American
       composer to deflect the academic German tide from
       the musical shores of this country." He calls
       Hill's <u>Lilacs</u> "the American 'Afternoon of a Faun.'"

B18.   Smith, George Henry Lovett. "Edward Burlingame Hill."
       <u>Modern Music</u> 16 (1938-39), 11-16.

       This short biography with selected work list is the
       only work devoted entirely to Hill's career and
       music. "Hill's music is not a reflection of French
       impressionism; it is an independently grown New
       England impressionism, derived from the ecstasy and
       color of the composer's native haunts. Reading back
       from the symphonies, <u>Lilacs</u>, and the late chamber
       music, one is impressed with the steady growth of
       this impressionistic technic, a growth through the
       Americanism of MacDowell, through the discoveries of
       the impressionistic movement, to a kind of speech
       that is at once American and individual, native New
       England and characteristic" (p. 14).

B19.   Spalding, Walter Raymond. Music at Harvard: A
       Historical Review of Men and Events. New York:
       Coward-McCann, 1935.

       This work is useful for the history of the
       department at Harvard. Spalding describes Hill as
       "a creative composer of imaginative power and
       achievement in several fields--an author as well"
       (p. 202).

B20.   Thomson, Virgil. American Music Since 1910. New
       York: Holt, Rinchart and Winston, 1971.

       Thomson dubs Hill "a sound impressionist composer, a
       master of orchestration, and a valued pedagogue" (p.
       151).

B21.   Thomson, Virgil. Music Right and Left. New York:
       Henry Holt and Co., 1951.

       Thomson describes Hill's style as "neoclassicized
       (if I may invent the word) impressionism" (p. 188).

B22.   Thomson, Virgil. Virgil Thomson. New York: Alfred
       A. Knopf, 1967.

       In this work Thomson notes his long friendship with
       Hill and recalls the influence Hill had on his
       career. Hill was Thomson's advisor and teacher at
       Harvard. "Orchestration I learned only from him"
       (p. 46), Thomson notes. He also claims that
       "through the views and musical ways of E. B. Hill,
       which were French to the core, I came in my Harvard
       years to identify with France virtually all of
       music's recent glorious past, most of its acceptable
       present, and a large part of its future" (p. 51).

Reviews of Hill's Book

B23.   Downes, Olin. "Modern French Composers." New York
       Times 21 Sep. 1924, X:6.

       "The estimates and opinions of Henry [sic]
       Burlingame Hill in his book . . . are not hearsay
       and are not the bland disguised quotations of the
       findings of other investigators. . . . He has placed
       each composer in his relation to his time and
       cultural environment, and has characterized his
       individuality as it bears upon his artistic
       product. Perhaps certain of these composers are
       treated more considerately by the author than they
       will be treated by posterity. . . . Mr. Hill is far
       too modest and experienced a critic to put within
       book covers partisan leanings or snap judgments of

contemporaries. . . . It is, on the whole, the most
comprehensive and authoritative work on its subject
that has thus far appeared in English."

B24. Finck, Henry T. "French Composers." Saturday Review
of Literature 1/9 (27 Sep. 1924), 144.

The book, according to Finck, "is indispensable to
writers on contemporary art and to all who wish to
be informed as to French music from the days of
Gounod . . . to the latest 'polyharmonic' and
'atonal' iconoclasts." "Much as has been written
about Debussy, the pages on his music in this book
are probably the most illuminating thus far
printed." Finck points out that some of what Hill
claims as French innovations actually first appeared
in Russian music. The reviewer also asserts that
Hill's descriptions of Satie, Milhaud, Honegger, and
other modernists may be labor lost, since these
composers "will never be greatly admired on this
side of the Atlantic."

B25. Prunières, Henry. Review of Modern French Music.
Revue musicale 6/1 (1924), 82-83.

Prunières offers a very favorable review of Hill's
book. "Je ne connais pas d'ouvrage consacré à la
Musique française contemporaine qui représente avec
plus d'impartialité et de compréhension sympathique
les diverses tendances de l'Ecole Française de 1870
à 1924" (p. 82). He notes one reservation: that
Hill accepts the legend of "The Six" and groups them
and other young composers into one chapter called "A
Group of Iconoclasts." Prunières does not consider
Honegger, Tailleferre, Durey, and several others
iconoclasts. He hopes that in a later edition Hill
will adopt another classification.

B26. Spalding, Walter R. Review of Modern French Music.
Crimson Bookshelf, Nov. 1924, 5.

"Heretofore anyone who wished to inform himself
about modern French music had to dip into books
which were widely scattered and which were written
in a number of foreign languages. Professor Hill
has presented with notable success the vast amount
of material at his disposal and has expressed his
views and estimates in such a way that every lover
of music cannot fail to welcome the book."

Reviews of Performances

Granada

B27.   "Fun at the Hasty Pudding Club Play." Boston Evening
        Transcript, 13 Apr. 1894, 5. See W39a.

        The reviewer mentions the "catchy score."

Jack Frost, Pantomime for Orchestra, op. 16

B28.   Hubbard, W. L. "Seein' Things at Night--The Musical
        View." Chicago Daily Tribune, 7 Jan. 1908, 3. See
        W36a.

        ". . . The music . . . would scarce have been
        written had not one Richard Wagner composed the
        'Ring of the Nibelungen.' . . . 'Jack Frost' can be
        described only as a pleasing, scholarly piece of
        writing along pronouncedly Wagnerian lines. . . .
        His whole idiom is Wagnerian, and yet he has so
        combined and written the different parts that he has
        produced a composition that is heard with pleasure
        and interest and that is effective and well
        illustrative of the scene it accompanies."

Nuns of the Perpetual Adoration, op. 15

B29.   A., P. C. "MacDowell Club." Boston Herald, 8 Apr.
        1936. See W44g.

        ". . . The simple, homophonic texture of the voice-
        parts, combined with a more impressionistic
        treatment of the orchestra conveys faithfully the
        spirit of the poem."

B30.   "American Music Society." Christian Science Monitor,
        19 May 1909, 7. See W44a.

        There is no specific review of Nuns. The reviewer
        describes the ideals of the American Music Society
        for supporting American music.

B31.   J[ansky]., N[elson]. M[oreau]. "MacDowell Group in
        Novel Program." Boston Evening Transcript, 8 Apr.
        1936. See W44g.

        ". . . Chorally, Hill does not write in the full
        harmonies found in the common stock of music, but in
        lines and planes and the color obtained from close
        counterpoint. . . . his musical setting seems rather
        restless and undecided."

B32.   "Modern Music Society Presents American Works." <u>New York Herald</u>, 14 Feb. 1914, 11. See W44e.

No specific review of <u>Nuns</u> is offered. Of the entire all-American program in general, the reviewer notes: "If none of the works gave evidence of supreme excellence, at least the general average was high."

B33.   "Music and Drama: News of the Day." <u>Boston Evening Transcript</u>, 19 May 1909, 21. See W44a.

"The programme . . . was well chosen and admirably carried out."

B34.   Smith, Warren Storey. "M'Dowell Club Concert." <u>Boston Post</u>, 8 Apr. 1936. See W44g.

The reviewer cites Hill's "sympathetic and appropriate setting."

<u>Pan and the Star, Pantomime for Orchestra and Women's Voices</u>
op. 19

B35.   C., P. G. "Music and Musicians: Mr. Hill's Pantomime for the First Time: An Interesting Experiment on the French Model." <u>Boston Evening Transcript</u>, 9 Dec. 1914, 22. See 37b.

". . . Not only is Mr. Hill's music always of great merit from the purely musical standpoint, but its dramatic aptness is extraordinary. . . . Here is a private citizen, so far as the stage is concerned, whose imagination and finesse of feeling are equal to the task of writing music for a stage action which shall at each moment be both appropriate and expressive. . . . Strong coherency and beautiful orchestral scoring bind together the several episodes into a fresh, vigorous and fascinating whole."

B36.   Kramer, A. Walter. "Peterboro's 1914 Festival Upholds Lofty Standards." <u>Musical America</u> 20/17 (29 Aug. 1914), 1, 4, 5. See W37a.

"Mr. Hill has given us compositions of individual stripe from time to time, but none that can rank with this masterly score. His work is conceived on a lofty plane. The instrumentation is gorgeously done, rich and sonorous where required and again light, ethereal and transparent" (p. 4).

<u>The Parting of Lancelot and Guinevere</u>, op. 22

B37.   C., C. "New Music by Mr. Hill." <u>Boston Evening Transcript</u>, 6 Jan. 1916, 14. See W4a.

". . . It shows study and assimilation. The
orchestration is original and sure. . . . In a
country yet uncertain of its musical orientation, a
few musicians have sensed the new and revivifying
currents that come once in so often to make our
jaded expression truer and fresher. . . . Mr. Hill
belongs to this small and distinguished group."

B38.   Downes, Olin. "Tone Poem by Boston Composer." Boston
Post, 25 Mar. 1916. See W4b.

". . . The longing theme of Guinevere, the knightly
music of Lancelot, are combined and developed, in
modern fashion, with the aid of the myriad colors of
the modern orchestra. . . . But the work as a whole
does not correspond to the best of its component
parts . . . . The music . . . remains . . . a mosaic
of small motifs, combined in sections, rather than a
continuous whole."

B39.   Elson, Louis C. "Symphony Concert with New Work."
Boston Daily Advertiser, 25 Mar. 1916. See W14b.

"Mr. Hill managed to attain good coherency in his
work in spite of much tortuous harmony. . . . There
was dissonance enough to picture all the shrieks,
cries and swoonings of the unhappy pair."

B40.   "Orchestra Gives Hill's 'Lancelot' Symphonic Poem."
Christian Science Monitor, 25 Mar. 1916, 17. See
W4b.

". . . Broadly speaking, Mr. Hill is the successor
of MacDowell. . . . He is not to be counted . . .
among those musical arithmeticians, those tone
cipherers, who have tried to evolve an American
symphony from new combinations of Brahms, Franck,
Strauss and Debussy formulas."

B41.   P[arker]., H. T. "The Symphony Concert." Boston
Evening Transcript, 25 Mar. 1916, 2:10. See W4b.

". . . Mr. Hill has written it in modern and even
ultra-modern wise." The "short and impinging
motives . . . are not developed and interwoven in
intricate polyphony, saturated with harmonic
elaboration or drenched in instrumental color in the
fashion of . . . the Straussian generation. . . .
Mr. Hill is learned and apt in the new manner. . . .
He may even . . . occasionally overdo it. . . .
Neither his motives nor the tonal fabric that he
thus weaves out of them awakens more than answering
comprehension in the hearer. . . . For long, long
intervals, Mr. Hill seems to be mentally working out
the emotions of Lancelot and Guinevere. . . . The
inevitable result is as cerebral a response from his
audience."

B42.   "Symphony Concert: Edward Burlingame Hill Offers New
        Poem." Boston Globe, 25 Mar. 1916. See W4b.

        ". . . There are ideas of pleasing, impressive
        character, but the orchestral treatment, combining
        harmonic and contrapuntal richness with clarity of
        scoring, the poetic quality released through the
        admirable instrumental coloring go farther to
        establish a romantic atmosphere."

B43.   "Symphony Plays Hill's Tone Poem." Boston Journal, 25
        Mar. 1916. See W4b.

        ". . . The ardor and the ecstasy were painted
        academically by the composer. The music did not
        suggest any great and glowing passion. Mr. Hill's
        success, in this instance, is rather a matter of
        technic than of temperament. The poem is expertly
        scored and in the latest style."

Stevensoniana Suite, op. 24

B44.   Clark, J. V. "Bauer Appears as Soloist at the
        Symphony." Boston Record, 29 Mar. 1919. See W5d.

        ". . . Possibly Mr. Hill has been a bit too
        sophisticated in his narrative, but these failings
        are rather the weakness of his art form than of his
        material. . . . The work in idiom, and, once or
        twice in melodic line, suggests now Debussy, now
        Ravel, now Puccini, but Mr. Hill is not a rank
        copyist."

B45.   Craven, Henry T. "Kreisler and Stokowski Forces
        Provide Memorable Work for Philadelphia." Musical
        America 30/26 (25 Oct. 1919), 8. See W5g.

        ". . . It reveals a pleasing gift of melody. The
        score has plasticity and clarity of form.
        Nevertheless the naiveté of Stevenson's flowing
        verse is rather imperfectly preserved."

B46.   Downes, Olin. "Novelties Played by Symphony." Boston
        Herald, 30 Mar. 1919. See W5d.

        ". . . At first hearing we liked best the Scherzo
        and the final number. . . . The lullaby seems
        sophisticated. The march has humor, but it has this
        quality in common with other of the four pieces; it
        seems a very big affair for so modest a subject."

B47.   Elson, Louis C. "Bauer Soloist on Symphony Program."
        Boston Advertiser, 30 Mar. 1919. See W5d.

        "The opening march seemed too strongly modulatory
        and too intensely modern in heavy scoring to be

fitting to an infantile picture, but perhaps it was intended for the children of giants."

B48. Hale, Philip. "19th Concert by Symphony." Boston Herald, 29 Mar. 1919. See W5d.

"This Suite shows fancy, delicate humor, true invention and no mean skill in the instrumentation. A full modern orchestra is employed, but not to stun and dismay. As is the case with Ravel, the modern orchestra is here used to obtain light, tricksy, and even gently emotional effects."

B49. "Hill Orchestral Piece." Christian Science Monitor, 13 Apr. 1918, 15. See W5b.

". . . The last [movement] seems by far the best written of the four. The lullaby is frankly in the style of the modern French writers, particularly Debussy."

B50. "Hill's Music Grasps Spirit of Childhood." Boston Globe, 29 Mar. 1919. See W5d.

". . . This sophisticated equipment, speaking through a modern harmonic and orchestral idiom, overtakes and does not lose a spontaneity as grateful for its unconscious, artless simplicity, as for its happy surprises."

B51. M., R. "The Symphony Orchestra." Chicago Daily Tribune, 20 Nov. 1920, 21. See W5j.

". . . It is a pleasant, if slightly soporific, example of music making by a composer who patently follows the older New England and less explosive fashion in American composure. Its rhythms and melodies are conventional, and it is possessed of much quiet and unpretentious musical charm. It is a sincerely sympathetic setting for the lovely excerpts from Stevenson's 'Child's Garden of Verse.'"

B52. "Many Other Concerts." New York Times, 18 Feb. 1918, 9. See W5a

"Stevenson . . . might have been surprised to hear 'A Child's Garden' of his sympathetic fancy put in a 'chest of whistles' of modern orchestration."

B53. McIsaac, Fred J. "Child's Verse a Symphonic Poem." Boston American, 29 Mar. 1919. See W5d.

"Mr. Hill has a talent for melody and a pretty sense of orchestral color. Therefore his 'Stevensoniana' is agreeable to hear and worthy of a place on such a program."

B54.   M[eyer]., A[lfred]. H. "In the Way of the People's
       Players." Boston Evening Transcript, 8 Jan. 1934.
       See W5n.

       "Felicitous invention marks the whole. . . . What a
       pity that these charming little pieces cannot
       receive more frequent hearing."

B55.   "Music in Boston." Christian Science Monitor, 29 Mar.
       1919, 11. See W5d.

       ". . . Only a few incorrigibly adult touches jarred,
       such as the sentimentalism of 'The Unseen Playmate,'
       a bit of which also crept into the Scherzo."

B56.   P., H. F. "Damrosch Plays Hill's 'Stevensoniana.'"
       Musical America 27/17 (23 Feb. 1918), 18. See W5a.

       ". . . The object is legitimate and promising, but
       the composer, instead of a set of authentic
       'kinderscenen,' has written four ambitious,
       sophisticated pieces, which might pass at a pinch
       for the work of John Alden Carpenter, modern French
       in harmonic contrivance, pretentiously and
       colorfully scored."

B57.   P[arker]., H. T. "Symphony Concert." Boston Evening
       Transcript, 29 Mar. 1919, 2:9. See W5d.

       ". . . In spite of the orthodox belief to the
       contrary, a well schooled 'modernist' like Mr. Hill
       is loyal and logical with form. . . . Mr. Hill knows
       the current idioms of Paris . . . but he writes in
       the suite in an idiom of his own--light, keen
       rhythms, delicate play of harmonies, modulations
       that are the fingers of fancy upon scholarship. . .
       . It deserves a place beside Mr. Carpenter's
       'Adventures.'"

B58.   "Rabaud Gives First Numbers." Boston Traveler, 29
       Mar. 1919. See W5d.

       "Hill's 'Stevensoniana' is interesting throughout.
       At last we have a composer who can see child life
       naturally, not one who has to force himself to the
       view."

B59.   Repper, Charles. "Hill's 'Stevensoniana,' Produced by
       Boston Symphony, Proves Delightful Musical Excursion
       into Childland." Musical America 29/24 (12 Apr.
       1919), 18-19. See W5b.

       ". . . Mr. Hill's orchestration exemplifies well the
       greatly improved technique of scoring which the
       modern composers have evolved for the expression of
       their ideas. . . . Mr. Hill makes his orchestral
       color transparent and luminous" (p. 18).

B60. Sturm, L. G. "American Music Exclusively at Ohio
      Teacher's Convention." Musical America 28/10 (6
      Jul. 1918), 35. See W5c.

      "An enjoyable feature was the performance of . . .
      Hill's 'Stevensoniana.'"

B61. "Symphony Plays Work Illustrating Stevenson Poems."
      New York Herald, 18 Feb. 1918, 2:7. See W5a.

      ". . . The work has charm of a dainty character. In
      spirit the music is related to the modern French
      impressionistic school. There is color in the
      orchestra and dissonance in the harmonies, but
      simple, clear melodies run through the score. . . .
      There are few American compositions that have the
      charm of 'Stevensoniana.' . . . It is simpler and
      more direct than two other suites of children's
      pieces heard at Symphony Society concerts, Ravel's
      'Mother Goose' suite and John Alden Carpenter's 'In
      a Perambulator.'"

The Fall of the House of Usher, op. 27

B62. Downes, Olin. "New Work Played by Symphony: Hill's
      Poem After Poe Given First Public Performance."
      Boston Post, 30 Oct. 1920. See W7a.

      ". . . Mr. Hill has achieved beautiful
      orchestration, distinguished alike by its fineness
      of touch and its certainty of method, modern
      harmony, a warm gleam of human, tragic beauty in the
      musical portrayal of the doomed Madeleine. . . . For
      us, the composition lacks the commanding force, the
      powerful stamp of an all-condemning fate which is
      inherent in every line of the legend."

B63. "'The Fall of the House of Usher.'" Boston Evening
      Transcript, 28 Oct. 1920. See W7a.

      Excerpts from both Poe's short story and Hill's
      program notes are provided in this preview to the
      performance.

B64. Finck, H. T. "Music: Poe-Inspired Music." New York
      Post, 8 Nov. 1920. See W7c.

      "What he set out to do Mr. Hill has accomplished
      with commendable skill. . . . Inevitably it is a
      somber tonal picture, of course, yet a surprising
      richness in subdued tints is provided by a clever
      use of celesta, harp, tamtam, and triangle."

B65. Hale, Philip. "Music Inspired by Poe's Story."
      Boston Herald, 28 Oct. 1920. See W7a.

Hale previews the performance, tracing other pieces
composed on Poe's works and quoting from Hill's
program notes.

B66.   Krehbiel, H. E. "Work of Boston Orchestra on Its
        First Visit." <u>New York Tribune</u>, 7 Nov. 1920. See
        W7c.

        ". . . The thematic material did not seem very
        pregnant, but it was at least plastic, and Mr. Hill
        showed ingenuity and learning in his moulding of
        it."

B67.   Parker, H. T. "Symphony Concert." <u>Boston Evening</u>
        <u>Transcript</u>, 30 Oct. 1920, 4:11, 12. See W7a.

        ". . . Mr. Hill . . . is studious of form; he takes
        thought, shaping, subduing it to his poetizing, his
        illuding purposes. Chaste, not wanton, are his
        freedoms with it" (p. 11). "Mr. Hill takes thought
        and perceives the necessities of such a tone-poem. .
        . . The listener's mind hears, agrees, responds.
        But the interchange, the process on both sides,
        seems chiefly mental. Does not a tone-poem . . .
        ask something more and something different?" (p.
        12).

B68.   R., C. "Bostonians Present American's Work." <u>Musical</u>
        <u>America</u> 33/2 (6 Nov. 1920), 6. See W7a.

        "Mr. Hill writes with Gallic clearness and artistic
        economy of resources. He does not paint with a
        white-wash brush, but rather makes every stroke
        contribute to the effect and be necessary to it."

B69.   Sanborn, Pitts. "Music: The Boston Orchestra Heard
        in New Music." <u>New York Globe and Commercial</u>
        <u>Advertiser</u>, 8 Nov. 1920. See W7c.

        "The burden which rests upon the composer is to
        evoke an appropriate atmosphere. In that Mr. Hill,
        despite some very latter-day effects of harmony and
        instrumentation . . . fails. . . . [T]here is less
        suggestion of the haunting figures of Roderick Usher
        and the Lady Madeline than of an extended flirtation
        between Stravinsky and a Waldteufel waltz."

B70.   "Symphony Gives Fourth Concert." <u>Boston Traveler</u>, 30
        Oct. 1920. See W7a.

        "The composition is full of the moody morbidness
        that characterizes Poe's writings."

<u>Nine Waltzes for Orchestra</u>, op. 28

B71.   Downes, Olin. "Highbrow Waltzes by Symphony." <u>Boston</u>
        <u>Post</u>, 25 Feb. 1922. See W8a.

". . . He has achieved pleasing instrumental
effects. He is now fanciful, now gracefully
sensuous, but he has written with more freshness of
invention."

B72. Hale, Philip. "16th Concert by Symphony: Famous
Schubert Work Heads Program--Excellently Performed."
Boston Herald, 25 Feb. 1922. See W8a.

". . . These fleeting melodies, often fragments,
often mere suggestions of waltz measures, are
harmonized and orchestrated with true French skill.
While there is an avoidance of the obvious, this
avoidance is not painfully achieved."

B73. "Hill's Waltzes Win Applause at Symphony." Boston
Advertiser, 25 Feb. 1922. See W8a.

"Though written in the unconventional manner
characteristic of the 20th century symphony works,
nevertheless these waltzes are not imitative. . . .
they are scored with admirable skill and ingenuity."

B74. Levine, Henry. "Two Symphonies and Visiting Soloists
Make Notable Calendar for Boston." Musical America
35/19 (4 Mar. 1922), 43. See W8a.

"They are extremely songful, at times even
rapturous; harmonically they are zestful; but what
is most arresting is their distinctive
orchestration. Mr. Hill has achieved a shimmering
orchestral color of genteel delicacy and
aristocratic refinement, an incessant shimmer and
glint in an ingenious play of timbres. This set of
waltzes created a very favorable impression."

B75. Parker, H. T. "Symphony Concert." Boston Evening
Transcript, 25 Feb. 1922, 1:10. See W8a.

". . . At every turn Mr. Hill avoids the obvious and
the conventional--without laboring too obviously at
that desirable process. . . . If his motivs hardly
arrest the ear, if his moods do not much quicken the
listening fancy, it is pleasure to hear the play of
his harmonies, the suggestion of his instrumental
voices. . . . Without excess, without eccentricity,
Mr. Hill clothes his waltzes in the present vesture
of Paris--and adds agreeable frills and furbelows
of his own."

B76. "Prof Hill's Waltzes Part of Symphony Program."
Boston Globe, 25 Feb. 1922. See W8a.

". . . They are amiable and pleasing light music,
skillfully orchestrated except for a use of
percussion instruments that fails to integrate them
with the rest of the orchestra. . . . They lack the

melodic invention and rhythmic vitality that have
caused Johann Strauss' waltzes to be popular for
half a century."

B77. S., W. S. Boston Evening Transcript, 23 Feb. 1922.
      See W8a.

      In this preview to the performance, the reviewer
      notes: "Frankly light and unpretentious, seeking to
      charm rather than to startle or impress, the music,
      through harmonic subtleties and orchestral niceties,
      contrives to avoid the obvious. Yet it is never
      finicky or recondite."

March for King James' Entrance

B78. "As the Nation's Pageant, Plymouth-Made, Came to First
      Performance." Boston Evening Transcript, 21 Jul.
      1921, 8. See W9a.

      "The audience . . . quickly broke into applause by
      the more impressive passages, when the full sweep of
      the pageantry's best effects were embodied in the
      procession of King James, in the March of the Dutch
      Cities, and in the final trooping of the colors and
      forces."

B79. Levine, Henry. "Glowing Music by Ten Americans
      Vivifies Pageant at Plymouth on Tercentenary of
      Pilgrim Landing." Musical America 34/14 (30 Jul.
      1921), 1, 2, 4. See W9a.

      "The royal march in this scene . . . is stately in
      spirit, rich in instrumentation, and inspiriting
      [sic] in effect" (p. 4).

B80. "The Pilgrim Spirit." Christian Science Monitor, 22
      July 1921, 4. See W9a.

      "This great processional was applauded again and
      again in its progress."

Stevensoniana Suite No. 2, op. 29

B81. "From Stevenson by Hill." Boston Evening Transcript,
      26 Mar. 1923, 6. See W10a.

      The reviewer quotes from reviews in the New York
      Herald, and the New York Times,.

B82. Jones, Isabel Morse. "Conductor Honored by
      Decoration." Los Angeles Times, 2 Feb. 1929, 2:11.
      See W10d.

      ". . . The music is whimsical, as the verses are.
      The 'Armies in the Fire' was embroidered with

filigree notes; 'The Dumb Soldier' was not so
interesting in its comparatively colorless sadness,
but the 'Pirate Story' had an American swing to it
that pleased."

B83.   Levine, Henry. "Hill's Second 'Stevensoniana' Suite
       Played by Monteux Forces in Boston." Musical
       America 39/23 (29 Mar. 1924), 23. See W10b.

       ". . . A fine sense of proportion and fitness save
       the music from the perils of over-statement or mock
       sympathy. A delightful fancy pervades the Suite, a
       fancy delicately stirred by the moods suggested by
       Stevenson's verses. Mr. Hill's score is rich in
       harmonic texture, in melodic charm and in piquant
       rhythmic effects. The work was received with
       unreserved cordiality."

B84.   M., S. "Carl Flesch Soloist with Boston Symphony."
       Christian Science Monitor, 22 Mar. 1924, 10. See
       W10b.

       "Mr. Hill . . . has written agreeable, although not
       particularly distinctive music, which he skillfully
       orchestrated. . . . They serve to pass a few moments
       agreeably, without leaving behind them a deep or
       lasting impression. None the less they display a
       certain whimsical fancy which is altogether
       delightful."

B85.   Parker, H. T. "Symphony: From the Ancients, from the
       Classics, from the Moderns." Boston Evening
       Transcript, 22 Mar. 1924, 1:7. See W10b.

       ". . . By predilection and practice, he shuns the
       easy and apparent modulation, the convenient
       harmonic background. Yet in this 'Stevensoniana' he
       neither over-labors his matter or over-subtilizes
       his manner. Now and again, he inclines to Ravel-
       like, even to 'modernistic,' procedures; yet he uses
       them in his own way. . . . Not within recollection
       has Mr. Hill written with such gusto as in the music
       from 'Pirate Story.' His invention is fertile. . .
       . For once Mr. Hill has seen and known, warmed and
       written."

B86.   R., P. C. "Hill's 'Stevensoniana' Colored by Poet's
       Fancies." Musical America 37/23 (31 Mar. 1923), 6.
       See W10a.

       ". . . At times the music seemed a little too heavy
       for the fancy, too grand for the miniature hosts
       seen in the glowing coals of the domestic hearth,
       but it was always good music. The best of the three
       pieces was 'The Dumb Soldier.' . . . There was a
       whimsical gesture, a genuine touch of R. L. S. in
       the legato melody, firm but plaintive. . . The suite
       is scored with fine skill."

B87.   "Symphony Society Ends its 45th Year: Damrosch Gives
       a Novelty in Professor Edward B. Hill's Second
       'Stevensoniana' Suite." New York Times, 26 Mar.
       1923, 16. See W10a.

       "Hill's . . . suite, for which the Harvard
       professor had to rise and bow thrice from an upper
       box, was . . . music genially melodious, graphic and
       enjoyable."

Scherzo for Two Pianos and Orchestra

B88.   Hale, Philip. "Symphony Gives Ninth Concert: Unusual
       Program Excites Large Audience to Warm Applause."
       Boston Herald, 20 Dec. 1924. See W27a.

       "Mr. Hill's piece is light and agreeable music, a
       little spun out, considering the ideas contained
       therein. If one asks whether it suited the supposed
       dignity of a Symphony concert, the answer would be
       that the applause incited by this Scherzo and Mr.
       Bliss's extraordinary Concerto was more enthusiastic
       than any that has followed a superb performance of a
       masterpiece for many months."

B89.   M., S. "Maier and Pattison are Boston Symphony
       Soloists." Christian Science Monitor, 20 Dec. 1924,
       6. See W27a.

       ". . . In this piece Mr. Hill timorously ventures
       into the field of 'jazz.' Again and again he begins
       a real 'jazz' tune, a real 'jazz' rhythm, and just
       as he seems about to throw all discretion to the
       winds, he suddenly . . . scuttles to cover. The
       effect is disconcerting to say the least. . . The
       'jazz' style . . . is essentially coarse. . . . Mr.
       Hill . . . may be pardoned this slight lapse of
       judgment."

B90.   P[arker]., H. T. "Symphony Hailing Mr. Bliss,
       Saluting Mr. Hill, Clapping Pianists." Boston
       Evening Transcript, 20 Dec. 1924, 1:13. See W27a.

       ". . . In the air are syncopation and jazz. . . . .
       Freely and aptly he scatters chromatic spice. . . .
       . Mr. Hill does not labor at an acquired idiom and,
       like Stravinsky or Milhaud, go stilted and
       ineffectual within it. No more is he self-
       conscious, either in condescension or in ambition,
       like this or that experimenter with jazz, from above
       or from below, in American music."

B91.   R., P. "Two Novelties on Symphony Program:
       Concertos for Two Pianos by Bliss and Hill." Boston
       Globe, 20 Dec. 1924. See W27a.

". . . As an attempt to capture the rhythmic
vitality and the artless melody of jazz it is
ineffective. Mr. Hill dabbles in the rhythms of
jazz without venturing on the remorseless iteration
that is the essence of jazz. He does repeat his
scraps of second hand popular melody, his themes,
until one is utterly weary of them."

B92. Smith, Warren Storey. "Pianists Jazz with Symphony:
       Maier and Pattison Play Hill's Scherzo for Two
       Pianos." <u>Boston Post</u>, 20 Dec. 1924. See W27a.

". . . Faced with a full orchestra and two pianos
besides, Mr. Hill seems to have been over-conscious
of the traditional dignity of his medium and hence
fearful of writing the sentimental melodies and the
obvious rhythms without which jazz is not jazz at
all. One eye, or rather one ear, Mr. Hill turned
toward Broadway, but the other, it would seem, was
on the Champs Elysees."

Divertimento for Piano and Orchestra

B93. Gilman, Lawrence. "The American Orchestral Society
       Makes Music at Aeolian Hall." <u>New York Herald
       Tribune</u>, 29 Mar. 1927.

". . . He has again amused himself by flirting with
Jazzarella. . . . He is admirably detached, and a
bit amused--we wish, indeed, that he had been a
trifle less casual; for his piece would bear
extension and development. We wanted to hear more
of it."

Lilacs, Poem for Orchestra, op. 33

B94. "Boston Orchestra Closes Season Here." <u>New York Post</u>,
       11 Apr. 1927. See W11d.

The reviewer mentions that the pieces was
"apparently appreciated by the audience."

B95. C., S. L. "Golschmann Plays American Novelty."
       <u>Musical America</u> 54/4 (25 Feb. 1934), 24. See W11j.

"Mr. Hill has achieved moods of much beauty in this
new work."

B96. Chotzinoff, Samuel. "Music: At Carnegie Hall:
       Boston Symphony Orchestra." <u>New York World</u>, 10 Apr.
       1927. See W11d.

". . . Unfortunately Mr. Hill's musical ancestry is
not New England at all. It is in fact Russian,
which accounts for the Slavic hues of Miss Lowell's
lilacs in yesterday's orchestral novelty."

B97. "Les concerts." La page musicale, 31 Mar. 1939. See
      W11q.

      The reviewer calls the work a "poème symphonique
      d'une jolie atmosphère idyllique."

B98. Downes, Olin. "Music: Boston Symphony Orchestra."
      New York Times, 10 Apr. 1927, 2:7. See W11d.

      ". . . Mr. Hill has seldom written with a surer hand
      for beautiful harmonic and orchestra effect, or with
      more sensuous impulse than in this new work."

B99. Levine, Henry. "Boston Orchestras Feature Native
      Works." Musical America 45/25 (9 Apr. 1927), 37.
      See W11b.

      ". . . His treatment catches the beauty, the
      aristocratic dignity, and the proud ecstasy of the
      poem. The orchestration is iridescent; colors are
      blended with finesse and delicacy, and, best of all,
      a lovely poetic theme winds its way to an ecstatic
      climax. Withal there is the poised judgment that
      avoids the pitfalls of suppressed under-statement or
      the untamed exaggerations of over-emphasis."

B100. N., C. H. "Boston Symphony Presents a Novelty." New
      York Sun, 11 Apr. 1927. See W11d.

      The reviewer dubs the piece "a finely colored,
      beautifully scored composition, full of fervor, of
      sensitive ardor and delicate feeling. In thematic
      material and instrumental treatment the work was
      hardly distinctive, but its workmanship in every
      department was excellent."

B101. P[arker]., H. T. "So Forward Toward the Jubilee
      Year." Boston Evening Transcript, 3 May 1930, 2:16.
      See W11g.

      ". . . Nowhere within recollection has Mr. Hill
      written with the spontaneity, the propulsive
      freedom, sounding out of 'Lilacs.' . . . It has
      begun and it ends with the fine-cut Gallic line,
      that may serve a New-England tone-poet. . . .
      'Lilacs' remains music of personal and poetic
      quality, of his largest, if not his finest, command
      of symphonic means."

B102. Parker, H. T. "Symphony: Symphonic Mixture: Bach
      and Honegger, Lalo and Prokofiev." Boston Evening
      Transcript, 2 Apr. 1927, 1:7. See W11b.

      ". . . The lilacs recalled as from far and she also
      who versified them; the tenderness that a true-born
      New Englander never will speak out--unless,
      perchance, music, or poetry, be his tongue."

B103. Rogers, James H. "D'Indy Symphony Shows Brilliance."
       Cleveland Plain Dealer, 25 Mar. 1932, 9. See W11i.

       "A well-written composition, not particularly
       modern, in the accepted sense. . . . It is pleasant
       to listen to, and has many attractive moments. Mr.
       Hill knows his orchestral choirs, and how to
       practice economy in their use, as well as how to
       unite them in a mounting crescendo."

B104. Rosenwald, Hans H. "Chicago Symphony to Play in New
       York During Jubilee." Music News, 15 Feb. 1940.
       See W11r.

       It "seemed to be fragmentary work."

B105. Schmitt, Florent. "Les Concerts." Feuilleton du
       temps, 15 Apr. 1939. See W11q.

       ". . . Plus sage mais peut-être plus poète,
       Burlingam [sic] Hill, s'il nous surprend moins, nous
       charmera sans doute davantage avec ses Lilacs tout
       parfumés de temps."

B106. Sloper, L. A. "Boston, Bach and a Jubilee."
       Christian Science Monitor, 3 May 1930, 7. See W11g.

       "A rehearing served to strengthen the pleasant
       impression made by this music."

B107. S[loper], L. A. "Boston Symphony Orchestra."
       Christian Science Monitor, 30 Nov. 1935, 13. See
       W11k.

       The reviewer dubs the piece "a charming work which
       deserves to be kept in the repertory.

B108. S[loper], L. A. "New Work by Hill Performed in
       Boston." Christian Science Monitor, 2 Apr. 1927, 8.
       See W11b.

       ". . . Mr. Hill's lilacs, we feel, grew not on his
       lawn in Cambridge, Mass., but in the Luxembourg
       Gardens. . . . There is imagination as well as
       logic. The harmonies, mildly acrid in the French
       manner, have the effect of a brisk breeze."

B109. Smith, Moses. "Unmixed Pleasure in the Symphony
       Program." Boston Evening Transcript, 30 Nov. 1935,
       3:4. See W11k.

       "Hill . . . is definitely a comfortable composer. .
       . . Like the source of his inspiration, Amy Lowell,
       he writes of good old New England."

B110. Smith, Warren Storey. "Composers at the Symphony."
       Boston Post, 18 Apr. 1942. See W11s.

Smith calls the work "outmoded."

B111. "Tone-Poem Features Boston Symphony's Last Concert Here." New York Herald Tribune, 10 Apr. 1927, 1:22. See W11d.

". . . He has written in this work with a sensitive blend of delicacy and fervor. This music has intensity of mood and imagery. It is poetic, richly fibered and it is beautifully put upon the orchestra."

B112. Williams, Alexander. "Symphony Concert." Boston Herald, 18 Apr. 1942. See W11s.

". . . It is very French in character . . . not a note too long."

Symphony in B-flat, op. 34

B113. B. "Music." New York Evening Post, 13 Apr. 1928. See W12b.

"This work seems to mix Boston conservatism and some of the color characteristic of Mr. Koussevitzky's old country, though quite subdued."

B114. Bennett, Grena. "Boston Symphony Offers New Work at Final Concert." New York American, 13 Apr. 1928. See W12b.

"The Symphony belongs to the class of music that is interesting but not especially important."

B115. Bronson, Carl. "Miss Anderson Wins Ovation at Symphony." Los Angeles Herald Express, 24 Feb. 1939. See W12i.

The reviewer describes is as "a brilliant arabesque of instrumentation which reiterates a great deal, but which is scholarly and energetic to a marked degree."

B116. Cushing, Edward. "Music of the Day: Edward Burlingame Hill's New Symphony is Heard." Brooklyn Eagle, 13 Apr. 1928. See W12b.

". . . We doubt that it will please the fellows of the League of Composers and kindred organizations. Its roots are too deeply struck in the traditions of the Nineteenth Century, and for all its avowed effort toward nothing more incriminating than the development of musical ideas, it has a subjective and emotional ring."

B117. Downes, Olin. "Koussevitzky Offers a Novelty." <u>New York Times</u>, 13 Apr. 1928, 30. See W12b.

". . . It is not easy to estimate this score; if only for the reason of its disconcerting simplicity and at least technical conventionality in expression. . . . But the immediate impression of Mr. Hill's symphony is of a work in which a man and artist draws constantly nearer to the core of himself. This score is essentially simpler in expression than any other of Mr. Hill's other scores that we know. . . . There is no thought of style for style's sake. . . . The first movement of the symphony impressed last night as the strongest. There is perhaps too much of one prevailing color in the instrumentation."

B118. Elie, Rudolph, Jr. "Music." <u>Boston Herald</u>, 27 Feb. 1943. See W12j.

The reviewer calls the work "favorable."

B119. Gilman, Lawrence. "An American Symphony Introduced Here by Koussevitzky at the Last Evening Concert of the Boston Orchestra." <u>New York Herald Tribune</u>, 13 Apr. 1928, 16. See W12b.

"Professor Hill writes music that is hearteningly free of the academic touch. His pages have zest, eagerness, color. . . . it pleases us to think that in this symphony by a New Englander, with its blend of zest and reticence, vigor and balance, sincerity of feeling and economy of speech, there is a spiritual counterpart of the New England temper. . . . This music is never sentimental; yet it avoids endearingly the cold and indurated triviality of those vacuous young zanies whom Mr. Barlow has so neatly pigeonholed as 'the comic striplings of music.' . . . If one may not call it breath-taking or momentous, one may surely call it tonic and sincere and craftsmanlike. . . . the audience summoned Professor Hill to the stage for his reward."

B120. Goldberg, Albert. "DeLamarter Leads Chicago Symphony." <u>Musical America</u> 52/3 (10 Feb. 1932), 29. See W12f.

"The symphony . . . proved to be a pleasant, well written work, possessing the rare virtue of brevity. The composer was present and was cordially received by the audience."

B121. Henderson, W. J. "Boston Symphony Orchestra." <u>New York Sun</u>, 13 Apr. 1928. See W12b.

"The themes are all clearly defined and their succinct developments have a straightforward logic

which is without bewilderments and may therefore
displease the skyscraper brows of advanced thought.
. . . [The] composition . . . is far from being
professorial."

B122. Lawrence, Florence. "Miss Anderson, Negro Singer,
Given Ovation." Los Angeles Examiner, 24 Feb. 1939.
See W12i.

"Mr. Hill has used dissonances and even the broken
and irregular rhythms of the progressive writer in
this work."

B123. M[eyer]., A[lfred]. H. "Concert-Chronicle: Mr. Hill
at Home." Boston Evening Transcript, 20 Apr. 1928,
18, 28. See W12c.

". . . Its themes show not only originality of
thought, but beauty of thought as well. The
orchestration is masterly and at times brilliant. .
. . Mr. Hill has written a work of importance . . .
a work which one hopes will not quickly be shelved
along with a season's other novelties" (p. 18).

B124. P[arker]., H. T. "Concert-Chronicle: Merit
Confirmed." Boston Evening Transcript, 1 Apr. 1928.
See W12a.

"In second performance before a second audience on
Saturday evening, Mr. Hill's new Symphony was again
heartily received."

B125. Parker, H. T. "Symphony: A New Symphony, Mistaken
Wagner, Two-Voiced Violin." Boston Evening
Transcript, 31 Mar. 1928, 2:16. See W12a.

". . . Mr. Hill's generating themes fall clear upon
the ear and quick to the mind. They have shape,
substance, plasticity, individual quality. . . . The
progress is coherent without labor; the form,
natural and sympathetic vehicle for matter and mood.
. . . Mr. Hill is no stranger to the processes of
contemporary music-making. . . . Mr. Hill has
assimilated a Gallic clarity; achieved his own
incisiveness of stroke; found the fortunate mean."

B126. Q. "Novelty by Mr. Hill." Musical America 48/1 (21
Apr. 1928), 7, 22. See W12b.

". . . It is straightforward music, clear, fairly
smooth and not unmelodious; there is . . . a
freshness of the out-of-doors. . . . to our
suspicious ears there was a breath of jazz somewhere
about, and just a slight flavor of several familiar
modulations which orchestrations of 'popular' music
have adopted and on which they have left their
stigma. A vast audience acclaimed Mr. Hill" (p.
22).

B127. R., P. "Paul Kochanski at Symphony Concert." <u>Boston Globe</u>, 31 Mar. 1928. See W12a.

". . . The first movement seemed yesterday the most interesting of the three in its musical ideas. The chief theme recalled to one listener the finale of Respighi's 'Pines of Rome.'. . . Mr. Hill is not a modernist, nor does he pretend to modernism of style."

B128. S., R. D. "Los Angeles Titillated as Film Diva Kisses Conductor." <u>Musical Courier</u>, 15 Mar. 1939. See W12i.

"It proved a work of engaging vitality, authoritatively scored."

B129. Sanborn, Pitts. "Koussevitzky, Distortionist, Takes in Hand Beethoven." <u>New York Telegram</u>, 13 Apr. 1928. See W12b.

". . . The listener easily detects the influence of Brahms. But music did not end for Mr. Hill when Brahms departed this life in 1897. Debussy engaged his attention and, later, Stravinsky. Here in the concluding rondo there is even a hint of jazz."

B130. Saunders, Richard D. <u>Hollywood Citizen News</u>, 24 Feb. 1939. See W12i.

"It proved a work of engaging vitality, authoritatively scored with a sound appreciation of tonal values and colors."

B131. Simon, Leo. "Anderson Scores Again." <u>Los Angeles Evening News</u>, 24 Feb. 1939. See W12i.

"His composition . . . is anything but pedantic. It embodies all the mechanical traits of modernism and is vital to the point of becoming tiresome."

B132. Sloper, L. A. "New American Symphony Has First Hearing." <u>Christian Science Monitor</u>, 31 Mar. 1928, 6. See W12a.

". . . He succeeds in employing a classical form without being dull, while his idiom leaves no doubt as to the period of his composition. Most remarkable of all the characteristics of this music is its melodiousness."

B133. Smith, Warren Storey. "Two 'Firsts' on Symphony List." <u>Boston Daily Globe</u>, 27 Feb. 1943. See W12j.

The reviewer describes the work as "soundly written."

B134. Stokes, Richard L. "Realm of Music." New York
Evening World, 13 Apr. 1928. See W12b.

". . . This work illustrates Mr. Hill's erudition in
orchestral writing, his stamina of personality and a
gift for serious if not profound musing in tones.
It depicted also his difficulty in conjuring up
motives of weight and substance."

B135. Ussher, Bruno David. "Music." Los Angeles Daily
News, 24 Feb. 1939. See W12i.

"Hill writes imaginatively, in a faintly celtic-
mystic vein when speaking lyrically."

B136. Weil, Irving. "American Symphony Heard: New American
Symphony Played." New York Evening Journal, 13 Apr.
1928. See W12b.

". . . The theatrical treatment the conductor dosed
it with made it at least seem to be alive.
Moreover, since it is cast in the pattern of nothing
newer than Brahms and Richard Strauss, it presented
no difficulties to an audience."

Four Pieces for Wind Instruments

B137. G., R. R. "Boston Flute Players' Club." Boston
Herald, 21 Jan. 1929. See W54a.

"He began with a prelude, rough-sounding to the
point of rudeness. . . an admirable prelude to the
elegant grace of the minuet."

B138. J[ansky]., N[elson]. M[oreau]. "Intimacy in Variety."
Boston Evening Transcript, 26 Apr. 1929. See W54b.

". . . Especially beautiful is the Elegy with the
slow melody and the mournful figures moving against
it."

B139. P[arker]., H. T. "Concert Chronicle: Triple Array."
Boston Evening Transcript, 21 Jan. 1929. See W54a.

". . . Mr. Hill sets [the instruments] to 'rough
stuff' through a sturdy Prelude; bids them diffuse
and sustain no shallow mood through the Elegy that
is finale. . . . Wit and fancy enliven their tongues
through the shortest of Scherzinos; while in
'company manners' . . . they walk the Minuet."

Ode for Mixed Chorus and Orchestra

B140. "Early Season in Bostonian Concert Halls." Boston
Evening Transcript, 16 Oct. 1930. See W47a.

The writer discusses the upcoming performance. Some
of Hill's program notes are quoted.

B141. Hale, Philip. "Music: Symphony Concert." <u>Boston
Herald</u>, 18 Oct. 1930. See W47a.

". . . In writing for the chorus, Mr. Hill treated
the singers as human beings with vocal limitations,
not as orchestral instruments. . . . Mr. Hill's
accompaniment preserved due proportion; there was no
attempt to outvie in strength and stress the vocal
forces; the accompaniment supported and
embellished."

B142. Meyer, Alfred H. "Henschel Returns to Lead Boston's
Symphony Jubilee." <u>Musical America</u> 50/16 (25 Oct.
1930), 3, 39. See W47a.

Meyer comments only on the "music aptly expressive
of that text" (p. 39).

B143. P[arker]., H. T. "Symphonic Afternoon of Rhythm."
<u>Boston Evening Transcript</u>, 18 Oct. 1930, 2:14. See
W47a.

". . . It shares no pigeon-hole with his symphony,
his tone-poem of lilacs, his two suites of
'Stevensoniana.' In one respect, indeed, there was
clear shortcoming. Mr. Hill is no instinctive,
adept or practiced composer for chorus."

B144. R., P. "New Ode Sung at Symphony Concert." <u>Boston
Globe</u>, 18 Oct. 1930. See W47a.

"It is only necessary to say that it was above
rather than below the level struck by most such
occasional pieces in the past."

B145. S[loper]., L. A. "The Boston Symphony." <u>Christian
Science Monitor</u>, 18 Oct. 1930, 7. See W47a.

"Everything is well put together, the accents are
precisely placed. . . . Yet we feel that Mr. Hill's
'Lilacs' and his Symphony in B flat will in the long
run reflect more honor on the Boston orchestra and
on their distinguished composer than this work."

B146. Smith, Warren Storey. "Second in Jubilee of Symphony:
Harvard and Radcliffe Singers Heard in Hill's Ode."
<u>Boston Post</u>, 18 Oct. 1930. See W47a.

"Mr. Hill is primarily a composer for orchestra but
he has written here gracefully and effectively for
voices. More mature singers would perhaps have done
his music fuller justice."

<u>Symphony No. 2</u>, op. 35

B147. "Boston Symphony." Musical Courier 103/6 (14 Mar.
      1931), 20. See W13a.

      "In this work, happily not pedagogic in spirit,
      Professor Hill does not attempt to say anything
      very novel or disturbing. His chief concern
      appears to have been to write workmanlike music
      which falls pleasantly on the ear, and this he has
      manifestly accomplished."

B148. J[ansky]., N[elson]. M[oreau].   "Professor Hill for
      Cambridge Hearing." Boston Evening Transcript, 13
      Mar. 1931. See W13c.

      ". . . Once attention had been gained and the new
      idiom accepted, Mr. Hill's symphony won every
      interest. . . . Gradually one was led to follow the
      new symphony as a stimulating intellectual
      occupation. . . . [O]ne noted the driving energy of
      the piece which kept the listening mind constantly
      alert and refreshed."

B149. Meyer, Alfred H.   "Symphony by Hill Given Premiere by
      Koussevitzky." Musical America 51/5 (10 Mar.
      1931), 4. See W13a.

      ". . . The harmonies are mostly of the accepted
      type. . . . The handling is always firm and sure and
      there are many felicities of orchestral combination.
      As a whole, the symphony will easily stand
      comparison with the best of contemporary European
      composition."

B150. P[arker]., H. T.   "Old Concerto, New Symphony, Rare
      Fragment." Boston Evening Transcript, 28 Feb. 1931,
      1:12. See W13a.

      ". . . It is a Symphony of this immediate day,
      frankly but not calculatingly modernistic; neither
      mannered nor opinionated; preferring the play of
      sonorities, rhythms, timbres to emotionalized or
      poetized expression. . . . A virtuoso-symphony--the
      listener repeated to himself. . . . Then came the
      reservations. . . . There are no marks of an
      environment and a soil; whereas Mr. Hill's first
      Symphony sounded out of New England; was seldom
      tuned to an eclectic modernism."

B151. Perkins, Francis D.   "Hill Symphony is Played Here by
      Koussevitzky." New York Herald Tribune, 8 Mar.
      1931. See W13b.

      ". . . Its musical ideas, indeed, do not soar to
      Brahmsian or Wagnerian heights, but the work merits
      a place well toward the front among the new music
      heard here in recent years, and deserves further
      hearing."

B152. S[loper]., L. A. "Boston Symphony Orchestra."
      Christian Science Monitor, 28 Feb. 1931, 4. See
      W13a.

      ". . . The musical ideas of the composer are
      characteristically his own, the idiom in which he
      conveys them that of the modern French school. . . .
      Rhythmic patterns are perhaps somewhat more complex
      than in the former works, but the influence of the
      modern Russians is slight."

Concertino in One Movement for Piano and Orchestra, op. 36

B153. "Concert-Chronicle." Boston Evening Transcript, 8 May
      1933, 20. See W29c.

      The writer offers no review of the piece but
      reassures his public that "there are still composers
      in Boston."

B154. Cushing, Edward. "Music of the Day: The Boston
      Orchestra at the Academy." Brooklyn Eagle, 2 Feb.
      1934. See W29f.

      ". . . One regrets the necessity of reporting it an
      unimportant piece--brief and qualitatively as well
      as quantitatively negligible. . . . There is humor
      in the piece--its single merit aside from its neat
      construction--but of a sort to remind the listener
      that Mr. Hill is and has been these many years at
      home in academic precincts."

B155. D., F. "Faust and Symphony Applauded in Brooklyn."
      Musical America, 25 Feb. 1934. See W29f.

      "The work disclosed an amiable interplay of
      whimsical humor."

B156. H. H. "Boston Symphony Offers Hill Work." New York
      Times, 4 Feb. 1934, 2:3. See W29g.

      ". . . It is gay and unpretentious music for the
      most part, innocent of contemporary dissonantal
      idioms and strewn with glittering and Puckish
      figures for piano and orchestra. . . . [O]ne felt
      that the material could have been better presented
      if it had been better ordered and the ideas, once
      stated, more clearly developed."

B157. "Hanson Conducts Eastman Concert." New York Times, 5
      May 1933, 13. See W29c.

      "Mr. Hill's admirable concertino, terse, of well-
      chosen material, reticent but forceful in score and
      finely played by Sandor Vas and the orchestra."

B158. Hooker, Adelaide. "Crusading for Americans at
        Rochester." Modern Music 10 (1932-33), 207-209.
        See W29c.

        "Hill's Concertino for piano and orchestra, though
        it offers no addition to our musical vocabulary has
        clarity and directness that justify it completely as
        music" (p. 208).

B159. Johnson, H. Earle. "N. H. Symphony Draws Big Crowd at
        First Concert." New Haven Register, 20 Nov. 1933.
        See W29d.

        The work "is full blooded and warm, with strong
        rhythms and modern orchestration; contemporary music
        in the best sense. . . . [It] might have been called
        the Rhapsody in Scarlet, so far does it surpass Mr.
        Gerschwin at his own game."

B160. M. "New Work by Edward Burlingame Hill for Piano and
        Orchestra Played." Musical America, 10 Feb. 1934.
        See W29g.

        "Mr. Hill's composition does not live up to the
        promise of its early measures, though it compensates
        in complicated rhythms and spasmodic coloring for
        what it lacks in thematic material. The work has
        the effect of modern jazz superimposed on French
        impressionism, demanding a brittle treatment by the
        solo instrument."

B161. McManus, George S. "Symphony Concert." Boston
        Herald, 10 Mar. 1934. See W29h.

        The work "is one of the really clever pieces for
        this combination written in recent years. The piano
        part is formidable and effective in the modern
        percussive sense."

B162. M[eyer]., A[lfred]. H. "His Concertino for Its First
        Hearing." Boston Evening Transcript, 26 Apr. 1932,
        16, 24. See W29a.

        ". . . It is tremendously vital and breathes the
        spirit of the day in which it arose; it is as
        bracing as a cold day in sunshiny spring. Further--
        which will be a point for many--it accomplishes its
        purposes without forsaking the paths of tonal
        pleasantness" (p. 24).

B163. P[arker]., H. T. "Symphonic Afternoon Variously."
        Boston Evening Transcript, 10 Mar. 1934, 3:4, 5.
        See W29h.

        ". . . The Concertino is a little miracle of
        condensation and cohesion. . . . From beginning to
        end it maintains itself in continuous and variegated
        development, both unlabored. The principal theme

interests in itself; in one phase after another unifies the whole Concertino. Not even in his symphonies is Mr. Hill more the ready and individual craftsman."

B164. P[arker]., H. T. "To Cambridge For A New Concerto." Boston Evening Transcript, 29 Apr. 1932. See W29b.

". . . He exposes a principal theme that accepts the contemporary convention of the piano as primarily a percussive instrument. . . . Mr. Hill has written a virtuoso-piece that is neither dry, mechanical nor cold-blooded; that he animates with spirited turns, or darts of tonal wit."

B165. Parker, W. J. "Boston Symphony Plans Festival." Musical America 52/10 (25 May 1932), 22. See W29a.

"The work, in three movements, utilizes attractive thematic material, and has a brilliantly written solo part. It is discreetly modern in its harmonies. The performance was warmly received."

B166. Perkins, Francis D. "Edward B. Hill Concertino has New York Premiere." New York Herald Tribune, 4 Feb. 1934, 1:13. See W29g.

"Excellently constructed from a formal point of view and ably orchestrated, the concertino makes a pleasing impression. . . . This work can be well recommended to conductors who wish to present a short piano concerto without having to resort to the hard worked Liszt concerto in E flat."

B167. Prentice, Thomas M. "Musical Moments: First Symphony Concert." New Haven Journal-Courier, 20 Nov. 1933. See W29d.

"The composition shows an excellent command of orchestral technique including variety of rhythm and tone color."

B168. S., S. "Music: Monday Evening Symphony." Boston Herald, 26 Apr. 1932. See W29a.

". . . Both the vigorous figure of its main theme (which reappears in various guises throughout the concertino) and its peculiarly brittle brilliance suggest the 18th century Italian harpsichord style. The harmonic idiom, however, particularly in the elaborately decorative development section, is of far more recent vintage."

B169. S[loper]., L. A. "Music: Final Monday Symphony." Christian Science Monitor, 26 Apr. 1932. See W29a.

". . . It has none of the impressionistic charm of the symphonies and the 'Lilacs,' but speaks rather

in the staccato voice of the modernists, though in
form it is classical."

B170. Smith, Moses. "Orchestra in Blaze of Glory." Boston
American, 26 Apr. 1932. See W29a.

". . . Structurally the work seemed to offer not a
flaw. There were some rude orchestral and pianistic
dissonances and what might be called rhythmic
dissonances."

B171. Smith, Warren Storey. "Hill's Work By Symphony."
Boston Post, 26 Apr. 1932. See W29a.

It "begins portentously with measures that vaguely
suggest the corresponding portion of Tchaikovsky's
Fourth Symphony. . . . there are hints of jazz in
the Allegro."

B172. Stutsman, Grace May. "Boston Greets Koussevitzky as
Orchestra Comes Home from Tour." Musical America
54/6 (25 Mar. 1934), 19. See W29h.

"The score is dedicated to Mr. Sanromá, whose
fluent technique and sympathetic feeling for music
in modern idiom made for a performance of some
'gentlemanly' jazz discreetly in keeping with its
Harvard University background."

B173. Will, Mary Ertz. "Premieres Given as Rochester
Festival is Concluded." Musical America 53/10 (25
May 1933), 16, 44. See W29c.

"Dr. Hill's Concertino is charming, crisp and
vigorous and full of sparkle. Mr. Vas brought out
the essential quality of the piano part in
delightful fashion."

Sinfonietta in One Movement for Orchestra, op. 37

B174. C., W. T., Jr. "Novel Concert By Symphony." Boston
Traveler, 11 Mar. 1933. See W14b.

"There was a soothing, self-contained newness, a
lack of blatant dissonance, surprising in something
so typically American. Definite rhythm, modified
dissonance and the diminished octave were to be
found, but there was no sign of great musical
character. A mildly pleasing piece, nothing more."

B175. E., A. [untitled] Berliner Tageblatt, 31 Mar. 1933.
See W14c.

"Die Sinfonietta Hills ist . . . in einem Land
romantischer Tradition beheimatet: blühend,
schwärmerisch, ein wenig tristanisch schwelgerisch
in Haltung und Klang, aber in der 'übermässigen'

Harmonik und dem Arabesken der Bläser auch nahe
einem orientalischen Traumland."

B176. Hale, Philip. "Music: Symphony Concert." Boston
Herald, 11 Mar. 1933. See W14b.

". . . Yesterday the slow section was the most
ingratiating. The other passages are scholarly, as
was to be expected from Mr. Hill, but one reasonably
expected a lighter touch, more piquant harmonies and
more diversified instrumentation."

B177. Jansky, Nelson Moreau. "Boston Composers Represented
on Programs Led by Koussevitzky." Musical America
53/6 (25 Mar. 1933), 23. See W14b.

"It appeared to be a terse, skillfully written and
stimulating work. Interest centres in its animated
rhythms and stirring climax. The instrumentation is
to a large extent individualized after a prevailing
manner, yet the whole composition contains the
distinctive personal characters of the scholarly and
sensitive Harvard musician."

B178. L., A. "New American Compositions Are Presented by
Sevitzky." New York Herald Tribune, 23 Apr. 1933.
See W14d.

"Mr. Sevitzky reserved his best efforts for the
'Sinfoniette' of Hill, but a good deal of confusion
resulted from his energetic conducting."

B179. "Leader of Orchestra at Met Honored in Europe."
Boston Traveler, 4 May 1933. See W14d.

The conductor Sevitzky is quoted as saying, "All
three [American pieces] were big successes. I am
happy to say that I noticed in my European visit
that there is more and more demand for American
music."

B180. Parker, H. T. "Boston's First Times." Modern Music
10 (1932-33), 219-223. See W14a.

The work "was written at Koussevitzky's suggestion
to condense into a brief, compact music the
evolution and successive moods of a full symphony.
The composer answered with thought and will,
resource and skill. But when all was said and done
there remained an occasional piece that lacked
creative warmth and imaginative impulse. The mind
was interested in Mr. Hill's readiness and
dexterity; most other perceptive faculties
wandered" (p. 222).

B181. P[arker]., H. T. "Concert of Contrasted Composers."
Boston Evening Transcript, 11 Mar. 1933, 1:4, 5.
See W14b.

". . . The music is consideredly, rather than
imaginatively, generated. . . . Modernisms not too
recondite or too insistent, spice it. If there are
hints of Honegger at the beginning, elsewhere there
is unalloyed and American Hill. . . . Lacking only
is the mood with which Mr. Hill usually and
variously impregnates his music. Not that he has
written mathematically or even drily, only from his
head into the heads of his hearers" (p. 5).

B182. Schmitt, Florent. "Les Concerts." Feuilleton du
temps, 13 May 1933. See W14d.

The work "est sans doute moins habile, moins
concise, moins solide de plan et de forme, peut-être
même quelque peu incohérente et kaléidoscopique en
ses divers mouvements trop mêlés. Mais elle
contient de la musique, en revanche, une délicate
sensibilité alternant avec de violents sursauts."

B183. S[loper]., L. A. "Boston Symphony Orchestra."
Christian Science Monitor, 11 Mar. 1933, 3. See
W14b.

"In this instance the touch of jazz is very mild and
inoffensive; just enough to connect the music in
spirit with the great mass of the American people.
The score is of course scholarly in construction and
orchestration, but it is far from academic."

B184. Smith, Moses. "Local Composers Honored at Boston
Symphony Concert." Boston American, 11 Mar. 1933.
See W14b.

"The structure is compact, the writing is neat, as
in Professor Hill's earlier compositions. . . . This
music is jazzy in spirit, but the jazz is not of the
blues variety."

B185. Smith, Warren Storey. "Symphony in Products of
Moderns: Hill's Sinfonietta for First Time in
Boston." Boston Post, 11 Mar. 1933. See W14b.

"The idiom is that of the modernists, but in it Mr.
Hill seems to say more than do many of his
confreres. In the succeeding slow division he takes
a step backward harmonically and writes music that
hints at but just misses sentiment."

B186. [untitled] Courrier musical, 15 May 1933. See W14d.

"Le discours y est tour à tour vigoureux, poétique,
lyrique et, finalement, rythmé à la façon des dansés
russes. L'ouvrage est très honorable. . . . Mais
l'originalité lui fait défaut."

Sextet for Flute, Oboe, Clarinet, Horn, Bassoon, and Piano, op. 39

B187. B[erger?]., A[rthur?]. "Sixth Ditson Festival Offers
      Four Programs At Columbia." Musical America 70/7
      (Jun. 1950), 3, 19. See W56d.

      "Mr. Hill's Sextet was the best made; for all its
      dated structural devices and repetitiveness, it had
      formal logic and well defined and contrasted moods--
      commodities shared by no other works on the program"
      (p. 19).

B188. Berger, Arthur. "Two Generations." New York Herald
      Tribune, 20 May 1950, 6. See W56d.

      "Mr. Hill's Sextet, Op. 39, employs the winds ably,
      and its Gallic episodes of tea-time music in a
      politely jazzy vein were entertaining. But there
      was far too much of the Brahmsian element."

B189. Downes, Olin. "Columbia Festival in Chamber Music."
      New York Times, 20 May 1950, 8. See W56d.

      "Mr. Hill's quintet [sic] is a pleasurable and
      admirably written score. There is no need today to
      acclaim him as a composer of knowledge and taste.
      The music has wit as well as fancy. Syncopation is
      employed in places with humor and gusto. . . .
      Nowhere is this less than well integrated and
      entertaining music."

B190. Frankenstein, Alfred V. "Festival at Pittsfield."
      Modern Music 12 (1934-35), 41-43. See W56a.

      "Edward Burlingame Hill's Sextet for wind
      instruments and piano had the virtue of making the
      very poor Mozart quintet which followed sound like
      another Jupiter" (p. 42).

B191. Goldman, Richard F. "Current Chronicle: New York."
      Musical Quarterly 36 (1950), 444-447. See W56d.

      "Edward Burlingame Hill's Sextet for Winds and
      Piano, although jolly in its opening movement, lags
      as it continues; it also had the rather great
      disadvantage of being performed at a constant mezzo-
      piano" (p. 445).

B192. H., H. "Trio by Roy Harris Heard at Festival:
      American Work Has Premiere at Mrs. Coolidge Concerts
      in the Berkshire Hills." New York Times, 21 Sep.
      1934, 28. See W56a.

      ". . . The work . . . opens with a fox-trottish
      movement wherein conventional tonalities are
      embroidered with cautious threads of dissonance. It
      would profit by much compression. Though scored

with the utmost effectiveness, its material, which
runs to gay rhythms, sprightly whimsy and idioms of
the 'hey-nonny-nonny' school, is too thin and too
picaresque for its length."

B193. Kolodin, Irving. "Pittsfield Redivivus: A Return to
the Berkshires." Musical America 54/15 (10 Oct.
1934), 5, 36. See W56a.

"The Sextet . . . was easily the most 'listenable.'
Hill has accomplished here very little more than an
'occasional' piece, but it is neatly written and
shrewdly scored. Profundities are wholly absent and
a definite air of gentility clings to the work" (p.
5).

B194. Kuppenheim, Hans. "Rochester Holds American
Festival." Musical Courier 129/10 (20 May 1944), 3,
13. See W56c.

He describes the Sextet as "a work rich in beautiful
melodies" (p. 3).

B195. Levinger, Henry W. "Sixth Festival of Contemporary
American Music Held at Columbia." Musical Courier
142/1 (Jun. 1950), 5. See W56d.

"It was a delight to listen to. . . . The work has
decided leanings toward French music of the early
20th century, but its charm, imaginative, piquant
rhythmical structure and harmonic color are
beguiling. Because of its freshness and elegance
the work of the 78-year-old composer made a real
'hit.'"

B196. Perkins, Francis D. "Berkshire Fete of Music Offers
New U.S. Works." New York Herald Tribune, 21 Sep.
1934, 16. See W56a.

"Mr. Hill . . . exhibited an unprofessional degree
of lightness and humor in his sextet. . . . The
four movements of this likable work proved deftly
wrought and adroitly scored, with a pronounced
melodic appeal and varied color. One or two
movements left room for a little condensation, but
in general the sextet was a notable example of
craftsmanship and instrumental knowledge
unacademically employed."

B197. Smith, Moses. "New Music and Old Heard at The
Festival." Boston Evening Transcript, 21 Sep. 1934,
13. See W56a.

"In four movements, following classical models,
Professor Hill employed suave or piquant melodic
material, apt and appropriate harmonic and
instrumental dress, and, in the slow movement, more
than a dash of modal harmony."

Two Jazz Studies

B198. Smith, Warren Storey. "News of the World of Music."
      Boston Post, 24 May 1936. See W15a.

      "Two of the four [piano duets] have now been given
      the dignity of an orchestral dress, which enhances
      their attractiveness."

Quartet for Strings, op. 40

B199. B[erger]., A[rthur]. V[ictor]. "Chardon Quartet
      Keenly Attuned." Boston Evening Transcript, 24 Jan.
      1936, 6. See W57a.

      ". . . This is . . . pleasant music, alive,
      refreshing, and remarkably uncontaminated by the two
      vices which render the effusions of many current
      musicians unbearable--prolixity and ponderousness."

B200. "Harvard Concert Honors Professor Hill." Boston
      Evening Transcript, 11 May 1940. See W57c.

      ". . . Neo-romantic in style, the second movement
      was intense and expressive music."

B201. Perkins, Francis D. "Harvard Men's Music Given at
      Tercentenary." New York Herald Tribune, 17 Sep.
      1936. See W57b.

      ". . . Of the two compositions [n.b., the other work
      was Carpenter's quintet], Mr. Hill's gave the
      stronger impression of individuality, along with a
      pervasive and appealing lyricism."

B202. Smith, Moses. "Piston, Hill, Carpenter for Festival
      Close." Boston Evening Transcript, 17 Sep. 1936.
      See W57b.

      The reviewer wonders "whether the music does not
      sound better in the original version for solo
      strings [than in orchestrated version, Op. 40a]."

B203. W[illiams]., A[lexander]. W. "Music: Harvard Chamber
      Music." Boston Herald, 17 Sep. 1936. See W57b.

      ". . . It is a work of considerable charm and
      excellent craftsmanship."

Sinfonietta for String Orchestra, op. 40a

B204. "Boston Symphony Closes Season." Musical Leader, 11
      Apr. 1936. See W16b.

"The work is in four movements, presenting beautiful music, skillfully orchestrated, in which the composer shows his knowledge of musical form and thematic treatment."

B205. "Boston Symphony Ends Academy Season Here." Brooklyn Citizen, 4 Apr. 1936. See W16a.

". . . The audience . . . had the opportunity, which they seized avidly, of applauding another man who ought to be more prominent in the music world."

B206. Brown, Ray C. B. "Postlude." Washington Post, 29 Feb. 1940. See W16m.

The work, according to the reviewer, "abounds in a quiet wit which evokes the smile of appreciation and not the shout of laughter."

B207. Buchalter, Helen. "Artur Rubinstein Wins Bravos Playing Chopin's Concertos." Washington News, 28 Feb. 1940. See W16m.

The reviewer calls it "a lovely work, soundly constituted in the conservative style."

B208. Burke, Harry R. "Waltz Program Again Pleases." St. Louis Globe-Democrat, 4 Feb. 1940. See W16j.

Burke calls the work "a portrait of the chuckling laughter and the mournful keening which go to make up a man's reaction to the mystery of life."

B209. Burke, Harry R. "Waltzes Abound in Symphony Program." St. Louis Globe-Democrat, 3 Feb. 1940. See W16j.

". . . It's not an American piece. . . . Even in the Allegro Giocoso with which it opens, the chuckling in the strings becomes a bitter skepticism not unakin to Joseph Conrad's tales."

B210. C., R. B. "For Music Lovers." Baltimore Evening Sun, 29 Feb. 1940. See W16n.

The reviewer describes the piece as "profoundly interesting."

B211. Chase, William T. "Symphony Plays at Harvard Fete." Boston Traveler, 17 Sep. 1936. See W16f.

"He writes clearly, concisely and knows how and what to say."

B212. Chotzinoff, Samuel. "Boston Symphony Plays in Farewell to Season." New York Evening Post, 6 Apr. 1936. See W16b.

The work "was not a bit of Americana either past or present, but just an old-fashioned suite of no particular clime or era. It is, nevertheless, a pleasant score in four well-contrasted movements, each cleverly made and honest, and respectable in feeling."

B213. Downes, Olin. "Season Here Ends for Koussevitzky: Boston Orchestra Concludes New York Appearances at Carnegie Hall." New York Times, 5 April 1936, N:7. See W16b.

". . . He does not attempt weighty things in a score which is the work of fine craftsmanship, and he stops when he has said enough. There is here and there a curiously Russian tinge to some of the themes, as in the theme which sings over a fixed figure for the lower strings at the end of the second movement, and a theme in the finale, suggestive almost of a Russian folk-tune. These are, no doubt, purely chance resemblances, and only noticeable if considered apart from the context. The work was well received, and Mr. Hill bowed from the platform."

B214. E., M. S. "Sinfonietta in Initial Rendition." Boston Traveler, 18 Apr. 1936. See W16c.

". . . Especially effective passages were to be found in the second movement."

B215. Eversman, Alice. "Rubinstein and Orchestra Share Audience Acclaim." Washington Star, 28 Feb. 1940. See W16m.

The reviewer calls it a "work of character and imagination, smoothly constituted and original in the balance of ideas."

B216. Frankenstein, Alfred. "Review Given of Harvard Broadcast." San Francisco Chronicle, 17 Sep. 1936. See W16f.

". . . He has never taken refuge in academic dogmatism, has always regarded music as a growing and continuing art."

B217. Gunn, Glenn Dillard. "Artur Rubenstein Heard in Concert." Washington Times Herald, 28 Feb. 1940. See W16m.

". . . Its technical aspects are scholarly, but it has elements of melodic inspiration that are surprisingly ardent and revealing to have had their source in New England."

B218. Haughton, John Alan. "Manhattan Musical Events." Baltimore Sun, 12 Apr. 1936. See W16b.

The reviewer describes the work as "rather charming."

B219. Henderson, W. J. "Boston Symphony Ends Series." New York Sun, 6 Apr. 1936. See W16b.

". . . It is good music, full of virility, sound in conception and execution."

B220. Hynds, Reed. "Golschmann Gives Sibelius' Seventh Brilliant Reading." St. Louis Star Times, 3 Feb. 1940. See W16j.

". . . The second of the four movements did have a melodiousness sufficient to redeem the others."

B221. J[ansky]., N[elson]. M[oreau]. "Koussevitzky and Orchestra Before Visitors." Boston Evening Transcript, 17 Sep. 1936. See W16f.

The reviewer dubs it "a finely made, persuasive and scholarly work."

B222. Kuppenheim, Hans. "Rochester Holds American Festival." Musical Courier 129/10 (20 May 1944), 3, 13. See W16o.

He describes the Sinfonietta as "a melodious work of rich content" (p. 13).

B223. Laciar, Samuel L. "Ormandy Plays Miscellaneous Program." Philadelphia Evening Public Ledger, 24 Feb. 1940. See W16k.

The reviewer writes that the work is "extremely well written, although the music is not very inspired."

B224. Liebling, Leonard. "New American Work Presented Here by Boston Orchestra." New York American, 5 Apr. 1936. See W16b.

"The 'Sinfonietta' is pleasant material with no intent to strain the ears or knit the brows of its listeners. . . . The spirit of Tchaikovsky hovers not far away from the last movement."

B225. Marsters, Ruth. "Symphony in Season's Mood." Boston Advertiser, 19 Apr. 1936. See W16c.

". . . Not only does it bear the stamp of the fine craftsmanship and taste of the composer, but is distinguished as well by originality and freshness of impulse."

B226. Martin, Linton. "Variety of Novelties Stud Phila. Orchestra's Program." Philadelphia Inquirer, 24 Feb. 1940. See W16k.

The reviewer calls it a "neat, spry, well-bred
number. It is as innocuous as it is well-
intentioned."

B227. Mason, Redfern. "First Week of the Berkshire Festival
      an Eminent Success." Boston Evening Transcript, 9
      Aug. 1937, 10. See W16h.

      ". . . It is music of a high seriousness, of a tone
      not alien from that of Emerson when he climbs the
      high top gallant of transcendentalism."

B228. Mc., C. "Group of Waltzes Played by Symphony." St.
      Louis Post-Dispatch, 3 Feb. 1940. See W16j.

      The work, according to the reviewer, "exemplifies
      the scholarly mind of the composer and his mastery
      of the medium."

B229. Penniman, Helen A. "Phila. Orchestra, Rubinstein Win
      Praise." Baltimore News, 29 Feb. 1940. See W16n.

      It is a work, the reviewer notes, "of definite charm
      and appeal."

B230. Perkins, Francis D. "Koussevitzky Heard by 5,000 in
      2d Concert." New York Herald Tribune, 8 Aug. 1937,
      1:16. See W16h.

      ". . . The flavor is not for the most part distonic,
      but it is not modernistic in the sense in which one
      is wont to regard this term as a synonym for
      harmonic acridity. It suggests rather that the
      modes of a far earlier day as well as harmonies of
      the present have been fused in an entirely
      homogeneous and personal style."

B231. Perkins, Francis D. "Shelling Ends Concert Series for
      Children." New York Herald Tribune, 5 Apr. 1936.
      See W16b.

      ". . . The first movement contrasts a sprightly
      theme with one of Viennese and slightly Brahmsian
      flavor."

B232. Q. "Novelties at Last Boston Matinee." Musical
      America 56/8 (25 Apr. 1936), 12, 29. See W16c.

      ". . . Well made, in a miniature fashion, clear,
      limpid and nostalgic, this transcription by the
      composer of his string quartet, Op. 40, has a fresh
      approach to an old style. . . . The first and last
      movements have . . . well bred harmonies to clothe
      up-to-date rhythmic fancies" (p. 12).

B233. S., P. "Symphony Offers Two Novelties." New York
      World Telegram, 4 Apr. 1936. See W16a.

The work, "skillfully written in four movements, made an eminently favorable impression."

B234. Sanborn, Pitts. "Orchestras in Fifty-Seventh Street." Christian Science Monitor, 14 Apr. 1936. See W16b.

". . . Not only were there masterly writing for strings and an unfailing command of form, but thematic vitality as well."

B235. Sargeant, Winthrop. "Music of the Day: Koussevitzky Conducts the Boston Symphony in Concert at the Academy of Music." Brooklyn Eagle, 4 Apr. 1936. See W16a.

". . . It set forth little that has not been said over and over again. The amiable and somewhat tiresome score was given a painstaking reading."

B236. S[loper]., L. A. "What's Going on in the Arts." Christian Science Monitor, 18 Apr. 1936. See W16c.

"The Sinfonietta is a characteristic piece, marked by Mr. Hill's distinguishing qualities of finished workmanship, clarity of design, taste and charm."

B237. S[mith]., G[eorge]. H[enry]. L[ovett]. "Music and Musicians: Introducing the Hill Sinfonietta." Boston Evening Transcript, 16 Apr. 1936. See W16b.

"As for the music itself, let an antithesis characterize it. Say that it is perfectly at ease in its sophisticated maturity and that it bubbles with a freshness that is nothing if not the freshness of youth."

B238. Smith, Moses. "Full Evening of Music from Native Writers." Boston Evening Transcript, 20 Jun. 1936. See W16e.

"The Finale . . . is Mendelssohnian."

B239. Smith, Moses. "Symphony Concert in the Best Koussevitzkyan Vein." Boston Evening Transcript, 18 Apr. 1936, 2:4. See W16c.

". . . The opening 'Allegro giocoso' is well described by its title. . . . I did not like so much the moderately-paced second movement, for the sentiment seemed not to ring true. But the scherzo . . . brought freshness again."

B240. Smith, Warren Storey. "Wide Range on List by Symphony." Boston Post, 18 Apr. 1936. See W16c.

". . . The first movement, oddly enough from Mr. Hill, is almost timidly conventional, and although

the work grows steadily more engrossing as it
progresses, it by no means possesses the interest of
its composer's other orchestral works."

B241. Smith, William E. "Flagstad Soloist in Philadelphia."
Musical America 60/5 (10 Mar. 1940), 6. See W16k.

"Hill's Sinfonietta . . . proved skillfully
constructed and afforded musical interest. The
scherzo and finale were especially effective."

B242. Strickland, Harold A. "Music in Review: Koussevitzky
Ends Season." Brooklyn Times Union, 4 Apr. 1936.
See W16a.

". . . The work . . . resembles, in style, the
'Nordic' symphony of Dr. Harold Hanson. . . . [The]
moderato risoluto . . . is an admirable bit of
contrapuntal writing with the composer verging
continuously on atonality but remains in the
traditional road. The concluding part is remarkably
reminiscent of the opening strains of the prelude to
'Lohengrin.'"

B243. S[tutsman]., G[race]. M[ay]. "The Berkshire Festival
Opens." Christian Science Monitor, 9 Aug. 1937, 10.
See W16h.

"Hill's little piece also came in for enthusiastic
applause."

B244. Stutsman, Grace May. "Closing Symphony Concerts are
Principal Boston Music Events." Musical America
56/9 (10 May 1936), 22. See W16c.

"Professor Hill has made skillful use of the larger
instrument at his command, but his material is
better adapted to the more intimate quartet.
Although the work was admirably performed, a
considerable portion of its individuality was
inevitably lost in the multiplicity of players. . .
. The audience appeared to the enjoy the little
piece."

B245. "Symphony's Program." Boston Evening American, 18
Apr. 1936. See W16c.

". . . The Sinfonietta is a beautifully written
work, evidencing both the taste and skill of the
composer."

B246. Taubman, H. Howard. "Daytime Concert is Held at
Lenox." New York Times, 9 Aug. 1937, 22. See W16h.

"The audience was not satisfied until the composer,
who was seated in a box, walked down the center
aisle and shook hands with the conductor. The

tribute was a signal honor for the only American composer represented in the festival programs."

B247. W., A. W. "Stravinsky's Symphony of Psalms Given by Boston Musical Forces." *Musical Courier*, 2 May 1936. See W16c.

". . . The qualities of neat construction, jocular mood, conciseness and vivacity . . . were appreciated."

B248. W., W. "Music." *Baltimore Morning Sun*, 29 Feb. 1940. See W16n.

The work, according to the reviewer, "is conventional, and, if not exciting, is at least pleasant and undisturbing."

B249. Williams, Alexander. "Music: Symphony Concert." *Boston Herald*, 18 Apr. 1936. See W16c.

". . . It is music in Mr. Hill's best vein, well knit and logically conceived, with a lightness of touch that is often missing in symphonic music."

B250. Williams, Alexander W.   "Symphony Season Review: Stability or Change?" *Boston Herald*, 3 May 1936. See W16c.

"Mr. Hill's Sinfonietta pleased by the urbane use of those qualities which Mr. Hill has always had, a sense of humor and the concise expression of his ideas."

B251. Williams, Alexander.   "Tercentenary Concert." *Boston Herald*, 17 Sep. 1936. See W16f.

"It was an honor to have his work alone of all Harvard composers played at these concerts, but an honor which was well deserved."

Symphony No. 3, op. 41

B252. Bernstein, Leonard. "Season of Premieres in Boston." *Modern Music* 15 (1937-38), 103-106. See W17a.

"Mr. Hill's symphony was conservative harmonically, and had more to say in the second movement than in either of the others, in fact, more than in almost anything else of his that we have heard. Its chief virtue lies in the beauty of the orchestration; this piece could easily supplant *Scheherezade* as a schoolroom model" (p. 105).

B253. "Divide Honors at Severance Hall Concert." *Cleveland News*, 24 Feb. 1939. See W17c.

". . . In the last movement Composer Hill won some
fine effects with his handling of the brasses."

B254. D[urgin]., C[yrus]. W. "Symphony Hall: Boston
Symphony Orchestra." <u>Boston Globe</u>, 4 Dec. 1937.
See W17a.

". . . The harmony is clear though piquant, the
melody broad and gracious, and the whole work flows
spontaneously."

B255. Elwell, Herbert. "Composer Shares Orchestra Honor."
<u>Cleveland Plain Dealer</u>, 25 Feb. 1939. See W17c.

". . . Hill seems not to have been disturbed by the
revolutionary trends of the first two decades of
this century."

B256. "Hill Symphony, Enthusiastically Received, Will Be
Repeated This Evening." <u>Harvard Crimson</u>, 9 Dec.
1937. See W17a.

". . . The second movement leaves one with a vague
sense of incompleteness, as if the point were never
quite reached, or as if the composer had momentarily
run short of ideas."

B257. Huning, Wilmar. "Cleveland Players Perform
Novelties." <u>Musical America</u> 59/5 (10 Mar. 1939),
20. See W17c.

"Mr. Hill was present Thursday evening and was
called to the stage several times to acknowledge the
enthusiastic applause."

B258. "Koussevitzky Presents Hill Symphony." <u>Musical
Leader</u>, 11 Dec. 1937. See W17a.

The reviewer notes "such significant content. This
symphony will stand with the best contemporary
scores. The slow movement was extremely fine."

B259. Marsters, Ruth. "Composer Hill Given Ovation at
Symphony." <u>Boston Evening American</u>, 4 Dec. 1937.
See W17a.

It "is marked by the fine workmanship and freshness
which generally characterize his works."

B260. Mason, Redfern. "Notable Chapter Added to American
Music." <u>Boston Evening Transcript</u>, 4 Dec. 1937,
4:8. See W17a.

". . . The work grows in grace and the feeling comes
over you that here America is standing artistically
on her own feet. Not that there is any touch of
local dialect. The composer's America is of larger

significance. . . . Hill has written a score in
which the American genius comes into its own."

B261. S[loper], L. A. "Boston Symphony Season Closes."
Christian Science Monitor, 3 May 1938. See W17a.

"None of [the novelties] had the appeal of the
other novelty of the year, the Third Symphony of
Edward Burlingame Hill."

B262. S[loper], L. A. "A New Symphony From Professor Hill."
Christian Science Monitor, 4 Dec. 1937. See W17a.

". . . There are echoes throughout of Mr. Hill's
predecessors, but this time they include references
not only to Gallic but to German and even Russian
styles."

B263. S[mith]., M[oses]. "Symphonies by Poot and Hill
Introduced by Boston Forces." Musical Courier, 15
Dec. 1937. See W17a.

"The new work turned out to be Professor Hill's most
pretentious and, on the whole, most effective
composition to date. There are occasional
reminiscences; but these are more than compensated
for by the composer's masterful handling of the
orchestral idiom."

B264. Smith, Moses. "Symphonic Retrospect." Boston Evening
Transcript, 7 May 1938. See W17a.

"Hill's Third Symphony revealed him in more robust
vein than did his previous works."

B265. Smith, Warren Storey. "Prof. Hill's Symphony
Performed." Boston Post, 4 Dec. 1937. See W17a

". . . Occasionally, though very rarely, the
pervading geniality of his music lapses into mere
facility."

B266. Stutsman, Grace May. "Boston Orchestra Plays New
Symphonies." Musical America 57/19 (10 Dec. 1937),
12. See W17a.

". . . It did not sound especially modern, although
it nodded to more modern harmonic devices. It had a
certain restrained humor such as might have been
indicated by the late George W. Chadwick, had he
lived long enough to have absorbed the newer
harmonic idioms. . . . If he became a bit
loquacious, his listeners, no doubt, forgave him on
the grounds of melodiousness."

B267. Widder, Milton. "Two Contemporary Musicians Share
Concert Honors." Cleveland Press, 24 Feb. 1939.
See W17c.

". . . In the third movement . . . the French
influence gives way to a Wagnerian approach and this
is the movement that is most alive and enjoyable."

B268. Williams, Alexander. "Music: Symphony Concert."
Boston Herald, 4 Dec. 1937. See W17a.

". . . The most individual movement and the one
which is also the most beautiful is the slow
movement. . . . The last movement, which is the most
brilliant, is rather surprisingly derivative of
Wagner."

Quartet for Piano and Strings, op. 42

B269. D[urgin]., C[yrus]. W. "Jordan Hall: Boston String
Quartet." _Boston Globe_, 12 Jan. 1938. See W58a.

". . . This Quartet of Mr. Hill is distinguishable
for its insistent but clear-cut rhythms, spareness
of melody and a transparent harmonic texture that is
reasonably dissonant."

B270. S., S. "A New Quartet from Mr. Hill." _Christian
Science Monitor_, 12 Jan. 1938. See W58a.

". . . Mr. Hill seems to have abandoned definitely
the Gallic impressionism, the pleasant fluency, the
gentle jocosity, the smooth and elegant facture,
with which his name in the past came to be variously
associated."

B271. S[mith]., M[oses]. "Boston Quartet in a New Work by
E. B. Hill." _Boston Evening Transcript_, 12 Jan.
1938, 12. See W58a.

"Hill's Quartet . . . turned out to be a fairly
obvious bit of writing, occasionally suggesting the
more intense manner of the recently produced
symphony [Symphony No. 3], as in the more robust
portions of the first movement, but more
prevailingly venturing nothing that could not be
readily digested at a single hearing."

B272. Smith, Warren Storey. "Boston String Quartet's Last."
Boston Post, 12 Jan. 1938. See W58a.

". . . Mr. Hill . . . has more to give us than most
contemporary composers, whether foreign or
domestic."

B273. Stutsman, Grace May. "Recitals in Boston are Well
Attended." _Musical America_ 58/2 (25 Jan. 1938), 14.
See W58a.

"A feature of the program was a first performance of Edward Burlingame Hill's newest string quartet, which was cordially received."

B274. Williams, Alexander. "Music: Boston String Quartet." Boston Herald, 12 Jan. 1938. See W58a.

"At a first hearing the first two movements struck us as the most rewarding when regarded for their purely musical and emotional effect."

Concerto for Violin and Orchestra, op. 38

B275. Bauer, Marion. "Howard Hanson's Third Symphony Played." Musical Leader, 9 Dec. 1939. See W31e.

"Prof. Hill's Concerto . . . is graceful, and musicianly, without bearing too heavily on modern idiom."

B276. "Boston Orchestra Premieres Krenek and Hill Concertos." Musical Courier 118/11 (1 Dec. 1938), 18. See W31a.

"It is written in a clear and relatively conservative style, full of rhythmic vigor in the first and concluding allegros, and it contains a beautiful flowing melody for the solo instrument in the slow movement. The finale is lightly touched with jazz syncopation. As usual with the music of Professor Hill, the violin concerto is highly polished, neatly constructed."

B277. Brown, Ray C. B. "Postlude." Washington Post, 13 Mar. 1939. See W31b.

". . . In his harmonic idiom Hill shows his knowledge of contemporary radicalism without endorsing it."

B278. Buchalter, Helen. "Young Violinist Triumphs in New American Work." Washington Daily News, 13 Mar. 1939. See W31b.

". . . The concerto is unquestionably destined to become a favorite, for it has elements of satisfaction for both listener and performer."

B279. Downes, Edward. "Music: Boston Symphony Plays in Cambridge." Boston Evening Transcript, 17 Nov. 1939, 20. See W31c.

". . . While it is not a daringly original or revolutionary work, it would not be fair either to call it simply eclectic. It has a definitely personal note, it is, of course, of solid musical facture and the orchestration is effective without being showy."

B280. Downes, Olin. "American Music Applauded Again." New York Times, 26 Nov. 1939, 42. See W31e.

". . . His slow movement is conspicuous for its admirably sustained line, and a pervasive and poetical mood. . . . There is nothing superfluous, nothing unrelated to the central thought in it, and it is so well done that the casual listener might easily fail to realize the fastidiousness of the choice of material and the fineness of the craftsmanship."

B281. D[urgin]., C[yrus]. W. "Music: Symphony Hall: Boston Symphony Orchestra." Boston Morning Globe, 12 Nov. 1938. See W31a.

". . . His work is polished and very enjoyable. . . . this concerto is not pretentious."

B282. Eversman, Alice. "Ruth Posselt Offers Brilliant Mozart Interpretation." Washington Evening Star, 13 Mar. 1939. See W31b.

". . . Less colorful in the first movement, he achieves a poetic mood of deep beauty in the second and a gay, carefree note in the third."

B283. Kastendieck, Miles. "Boston Symphony Plays at Academy." Brooklyn Eagle, 25 Nov. 1939. See W31d.

"It is surprisingly academic, a little stiff, and more technically than aurally pleasing."

B284. Kastendieck, Miles. "Ormandy Inaugurates Rachmaninoff Cycle." Brooklyn Eagle, 27 Nov. 1939. See W31c.

The reviewer cites "expert craftsmanship without much spontaneity."

B285. Kolodin, Irving. "Bostonians Give More New Works." New York Sun, 27 Nov. 1939. See W31e.

". . . There was an unusual refinement of feeling in its materials."

B286. Marsters, Ruth. "Koussevitzky Back in Sellout; Ballet Russe Twists Beethoven." Boston American, 12 Nov. 1938. See W31a.

". . . The concerto obviously does not represent Hill at his best, despite moments of lyric poetry. The spontaneity . . . is not in evidence."

B287. Perkins, Francis D. "Koussevitzky Ends Programs By

Americans." <u>New York Herald Tribune</u>, 26 Nov. 1939, 32. See W31e.

". . . The first movement, which, up to the cadenza, treated the violin somewhat less lyrically, was also appealing, suggesting a post-romantic atmosphere combined with a little discreet polytonality. The brief finale left a certain sense of incompletion."

B288. Sanborn, Pitts. "American Music." <u>New York World Telegram</u>, 26 Nov. 1939. See W31e.

"Besides an appealing slow movement the work communicates little."

B289. Sloper, L. A. "The Boston Symphony Season." <u>Christian Science Monitor</u>, 29 Apr. 1939. See W31a.

"The slow movement charmed by its lyricism, its piquant harmonies, and its instrumental colors, but otherwise the work was disappointing."

B290. Sloper, L. A. "Progress of the Boston Symphony." <u>Christian Science Monitor</u>, 14 Jan. 1939. See W31a.

The work "was disappointing. . . . The opening movement is unviolinistic and choppy."

B291. Smith, George Henry Lovett. "Boston News." <u>Modern Music</u> 16 (1938-39), 114-116. See W31a.

". . . a work of simplicity and eloquence. The new clarity of style and the familiar wit and effectiveness of orchestration are ideally suited to the form of the violin concerto, which he handles with ease. The slow movement possesses a richness and depth of feeling infrequently found in contemporary American composers" (p. 115).

B292. Smith, Moses. "Symphony Concert," <u>Boston Evening Transcript</u>, 12 Nov. 1938, 3:6. See W31a.

". . . Here and there the composer pays the expected obeisance to the more or less traditional form and manner of violin concertos. . . . Much more often is the expression of an urbane, rather than a rugged, humor. . . . the slow movement of the concerto . . . is the most successful of the three."

B293. Smith, Moses. "Week-End Concert." <u>Boston Evening Transcript</u>, 14 Nov. 1938. See W31a.

"It is neither an important work nor a dull one. It reveals anew and greatfully the familiar lyrical vein of the composer."

B294. Stutsman, Grace May. "Two New Concertos Played in

Boston." <u>Musical America</u> 58/18 (25 Nov. 1938), 22.
See W31a.

"The first movement, despite some syncopated
rhythms, does not step off spontaneously. In his
attempt to produce an unstereotyped work, he too
obviously reveals that attempt, with the result that
the measures are more of a potpourri of harmonic
examples and various rhythms, than a really
homogeneous blending of thematic material undeniably
original. The composer no doubt feels more
sympathetic toward the newer methods of approaching
harmonic structure than he is able to make evident
in his music. The concerto succeeds, not in being
'modern' but self-conscious."

B295. T.   "Koussevitzky's Bostonians Give Second American
Program." <u>Musical America</u> 59/19 (10 Dec. 1939), 27.
See W31e.

". . . The concerto 'comes off,' particularly the
poetic slow movement. It has the structural
firmness, the clarity of scoring and the freedom
from extraneous clutter expected of this composer."

B296. Wheelwright, D. Sterling.   "Washington Hears Local
Organizations." <u>Music News</u>, 6 Apr. 1939. See W31b.

"The first movement suggests the folk dances of the
southwest; the second is reminiscent of the Debussy
touch, and the third gives a jazz touch that must be
native American."

B297. Williams, Alexander.   "Music." <u>Boston Herald</u>, 12 Nov.
1938. See W31a.

". . . Mr. Hill does not succeed in making plausible
or effective the contrasts in mood between the
jocose and the rhapsodic."

<u>Concertino for String Orchestra</u>, op. 46

B298. Downes, Edward.   "20th-Century Music." <u>Boston Evening
Transcript</u>, 20 Apr. 1940, 3:6. See W19a.

". . . There is true gaiety and urbanity in his
opening allegro giocoso. If the whole does not
attempt to scale Olympian heights nor to explore the
deepest emotions, it is always inventive and
consistently entertaining."

B299. Durgin, Cyrus W.   "Hindemith Violin Concerto in
American Bow at Boston." <u>Musical Courier</u> 121/9 (1
May 1940), 27. See W19a

"Since the first movement strongly suggests the
Classical Symphony of Prokofieff, and the main

theme of the second is conspicuously Tchaikovsky-
esque, it is logical to describe the Concertino as
more charming than original. The harmonic treatment
is tangibly modern, and so is the expert scoring."

B300. D[urgin]., C[yrus]. W. "Symphony Hall: Boston
Symphony Orchestra." Boston Daily Globe, 20 Apr.
1940. See W19a.

The reviewer describes the work as "more sparkling
than original."

B301. Gaffney, Leo. "The Symphony Concert." Boston
Advertiser, 21 Apr. 1940. See W19a.

The work was "less exciting, perhaps [than the
Hindemith Concerto], but ever so much easier to
listen to."

B302. "Musical Treat of the Season." Boston Post, 20 Apr.
1940. See W19a.

The reviewer describes it as a "generally successful
and frequently highly diverting composition."

B303. Sloper, L. A. "The Boston Symphony Season."
Christian Science Monitor, 4 May 1940. See W19a.

". . . If it could have been heard with less
overwhelming competition [Hindemith's Violin
Concerto], it would have appealed more clearly as
the charming slight piece that it is."

B304. Smith, George Henry Lovett. "Boston Premieres."
Modern Music 17 (1939-40), 254-255. See W19a.

". . . It is alert, eager music, full of vigor and
that elusive quality we know as charm. As always
the composer's workmanship is impeccable, his
scoring expert, his material suitable to the point
of distinction. This is music that is scholarly
without being cerebral; it is keenly alive--musique
du monde, to paraphrase an epithet" (pp. 254-255).

B305. Stutsman, Grace May. "Boston Symphony Offers Bach
Mass." Musical America 60/9 (10 May 1940), 15. See
W19a.

"Professor Hill . . . has written a pleasant
sounding little work for strings. . . . Since the
composition makes no extensive claim for this new
opus, one may not be too critical of it in regard to
measured balance between movements and the thematic
material employed. . . The Andante . . . seemed to
be a little expansive. . . . The concertino was
given a cordial reception."

B306. Williams, Alexander. "Music: Symphony Concert."
        Boston Herald, 20 Apr. 1940. See W19a.

        The reviewer calls it an "exceptionally attractive
        and ingratiating work."

Music for English Horn and Orchestra, op. 50

B307. Durgin, Cyrus. "Music: Symphony Hall: Boston
        Symphony Orchestra." Boston Globe, 3 Mar. 1945.
        See W33a.

        ". . . The style derives from late Impressionism;
        the orchestration is very delicate and prismatically
        colored, always allowing the foreground to the solo
        instrument."

B308. Elie, Rudolph, Jr. "Music: Symphony Concert."
        Boston Herald, 3 Mar. 1945. See W33a.

        ". . . And this quiet, nostalgic and cultivated
        music was eminently proper to the occasion, and it
        was wonderfully played by the soloist."

B309. Sloper, L. A. "Casadésus and Speyer Soloists With
        Symphony." Christian Science Monitor, 3 Mar. 1945,
        4. See W33a.

        The reviewer describes the piece as "an exquisite
        expression of the Gallic spirit, delicate,
        charming, restrained."

B310. Smith, Warren Storey. "Symphony Concert." Boston
        Post, 8 Jan. 1949. See W33b.

        The work "is uttering charming. . . . After the
        trenchant music of Harris, these soothing pages were
        welcome."

B311. Stutsman, Grace May. "Casadesus Plays Mozart
        Concerto." Musical America 65/5 (25 Mar. 1945), 14.
        See W33a.

        "Mr. Hill's newest work . . . is delicate and
        charming. Mr. Koussevitzky achieved an extremely
        sensitive orchestral background for the solo
        instrument which, in Speyer's hands, spoke
        eloquently."

Prelude for Orchestra

B312. Downes, Olin. "New Music Heard under Bernstein: He
        Conducts 10th Anniversary Concert of Koussevitzky
        Foundation at Town Hall." New York Times, 30 Mar.
        1953, 26. See W24a.

". . . The music is distinguished by the admirable
taste, sensitiveness, feeling for form and instinct
for fine orchestral coloring that have long
distinguished Mr. Hill as a composer. It is
essentially inspiration of the period of Fauré,
Debussy and Strauss. . . . it is incorrigibly
'romantic' and sensuous in its connotations. It is
also modest, which cannot be said of all the music
that was heard. Mr. Hill, in earlier years an
advanced modernist, is now retrospective of earlier
aspects of beauty and emotion keenly remembered and
truly felt."

B313. F., W. "Koussevitzky Music Foundation, Town Hall,
March 29, 3:00." Musical America 73/6 (15 Apr.
1953), 22. See W24a.

"A respectably academic, even nostalgic, Prelude by
Edward Burlingame Hill opened the program."

B314. Fried, Alexander. "Mixed Results of Oakland Mixture."
San Francisco Examiner, 22 Oct. 1975, 31. See W24b.

"His 'Prelude' exemplified the fact he was
influenced by French impressionistic music. It is a
merely mild work."

B315. L[evinger]., H[enry]. W. "Koussevitzky Foundation
Memorial Concert." Musical Courier 147/8 (15 Apr.
1953), 14. See W24a.

". . . It is a colorful score, written in the vein
of French impressionistic music, with a dash of
Richard Strauss' melodic structure."

B316. Tircuit, Henwell. "Performance to be Conjured With."
San Francisco Chronicle, 23 Oct. 1975, 43. See
W24b.

"Contrary to the date of its writing, the Hill work
is a Victorian color piece rather close in mood and
style to the music of Delius. . . . it is music of
modest goals, and indeed, modest attainment."

Reviews of Recordings

Sextet for Flute, Oboe, Clarinet, Horn, Bassoon, and
        Piano, op. 39

B317. Babbitt, Milton. "Musical America's Several
Generations." Saturday Review, 3 Mar. 1954, 36.
See D3.

"Hill's Sextet . . . recalls the problems and attitudes of that generation which, for the most part, resigned itself to the geographical fortuity of being 'outsiders,' and thus to the pursuit of literal identification with the traditional. The Sextet is a skilful synthesis of materials that evoke various aspects of early twentieth-century French composition, contained within somewhat disparately rigid external forms."

B318. Daniel, Oliver. "New Recordings." American Composers Alliance Bulletin 4/2 (1954), 14-21. See D3.

"It is highly agreeable music, but sounds strangely remote after hearing the work of most of our contemporary writers" (p. 19).

B319. Frankenstein, Alfred. "Columbia's Contemporaries-- 1955." High Fidelity 4/2 (Apr. 1954), 44-45. See D3.

"Hill belongs to an older school, the school of those who taught the pioneers and some of the younger men in American universities during the earlier decades of this century. The school is almost completely neglected so far as performance and recording is concerned. Its members are forgotten men of twentieth century American music, and it is good to see at least one of them included here" (p. 44).

B320. Haggin, B. H. "Records." The Nation 178/20 (15 May 1954), 431. See D3.

"The Hill piece is an evocation of facile French writing of fifty years ago."

B321. Lyons, James. "Americana." American Record Guide 20 (1953-54), 251-252. See D3.

"E. B. Hill's Sextet . . . evokes nothing if not the ever so polite astringency of Fauré and his coterie" (p. 251).

B322. Persichetti, Vicent. Review of the "Modern American Music Series, Columbia Masterworks." Musical Quarterly 40 (1954), 471-476. See D3.

"In direct contrast to the Ives [Sonata] is the retiring and amiable Hill Sextet, which follows a cautious European path and is most noteworthy for its shift from the Germanic tradition" (p. 473).

B323. Schonberg, Harold C. "Records: American Chamber Music is Heard on Elaborate Series." New York Times, 14 March 1954, X:8. See D3.

He mentions only "the dated French qualities (Fauré, Les Six) of Hill's Sextet."

Prelude for Orchestra

B324. Review of "Columbia's Modern American Music Series." _Musical Quarterly_ 41 (1955), 551-555. See D2.

"The Prelude . . . is attractive in its elegance and unpretentious facture, idyllic in mood, and sounds like the work of a more robust Griffes" (p. 555).

B325. Frankenstein, Alfred. "Columbia and the Contemporaries--1955." _High Fidelity_ 5/7 (Sep. 1955), 57-59. See D2.

"The Hill is a rather curious affair, warmly romantic, at times saccharine, but extremely broad and inventive in its harmonic palette and its orchestral devices. It reminds us that the career of Edward Burlingame Hill has spanned the decades from MacDowell to Schoenberg" (p. 59).

B326. Haggin, B. H. "Records." _The Nation_ 181/6 (6 Aug. 1955), 122. See D2.

"Edward Burlingame Hill's Prelude is a luxuriant exercise in a borrowed style of the past."

B327. Lyons, James. "Americana from Columbia." _American Record Guide_ 21 (1954-55), 383-386. See D2.

"E. B. Hill's _Prelude_ of 1953 is an unreconstructed Harvard gentleman's sensuous distillate of impressionate sensuality. The Debussy and Delius fibers are skillfully woven into a distinctive cloth and impeccably tailored into a fine conservative suiting. The sobriety is not as innocuous as you might imagine. Would that we had more of such unpretentious music-making, so sensible in its directness and yet so subtle in its understatement" (p. 386).

B328. Schonberg, Harold C. "Records: Contemporary Americans." _New York Times_, 10 Jul. 1955, X:12. See D2.

He mentions "Hill's pleasant, old-fashioned _Prelude for Orchestra_."

Discography

This chapter provides a list of all commercially produced discs, whether or not they are currently available. Each disc is denoted with an identifying label beginning with the letter "D". Citations are cross-referenced with with appropriate entries in the "Bibliography of Writings about Hill" ("B") and "Works and Performances" ("W") chapters: for example, "See W40" refers the reader to the "Works and Performances" chapter, item 40.

D1.   <u>Stevensoniana Suite</u>. See W5.

       Royal Philharmonic Orchestra, Karl Krueger,
          conductor.
       Society for the Preservation of the American Musical
          Heritage, MIA 142, 1969.

D2.   <u>Prelude for Orchestra</u>. See W24, B324-B328.

       Columbia Symphony Orchestra, Leonard Bernstein,
          conductor.
       Columbia ML4996, 1955.

D3.   <u>Sextet for Piano and Winds</u>. See W56, B317-B323.

       Lilian Kalir, piano, New York Woodwind Quintet.
       Columbia ML4846, 1954, 1968, 1974.

Appendix I:
Archival Sources

The Library of the American Academy and Institute of Arts
and Letters, New York.

> Hill having been a member of the Institute from 1916
> until his death, the Library houses many materials
> relating to him, including one score (holograph);
> thirty-six letters to Hill; and forty-five letters
> from Hill.

Boston Public Library, Special Music Collections, Rare Books
and Manuscripts, Boston.

> The Library owns one full score holograph, several
> letters, and three one-page manuscripts (holograph)
> with themes from various works by Hill.

Gorno Memorial Music Library, Conservatory of Music,
University of Cincinnati, Cincinnati.

> Eleven manuscripts (all holograph) are housed here.

Harvard University Archives, Harvard University, Cambridge.

> University course catalogs and other university
> publications as well as records from the Music
> Department--such as minutes of departmental
> meetings, correspondence of the department, and
> informational releases--are preserved in the
> Archives.

Houghton Library, Harvard University, Cambridge.

>The largest collection of materials on Hill is housed here. It includes ten large cartons (as yet uncatalogued) of his compositions (mostly holograph) and a number of letters to and from him.

New England Conservatory of Music, Harriet M. Spaulding Library, Boston.

>Fourteen manuscripts of Hill's compositions, mostly holograph, are located here.

Appendix II:
Alphabetical Listing
of Original
Compositions

3 Line Piece for Esther Hill, W92.
'94 Fox Trot, W100.

After Sunset, W134.
All's Well, W119.
And the Wilderness Shall Rejoice, W46.
Armies in the Fire, W101.
At the Grave of a Hero, W76
Autumn Twilight for Soprano and Orchestra, W41.
Autumn Twilight for Soprano and Orchestra (arr. soprano and
    piano duet), W152.

Bagatelle for Piano, W88.
The Ballad of Sir Guy for Voice and Orchestra, W43.
Beside the Idle Summer Sea, W132.
By Loe Pool, W143.

Chimes, W86.
Concertino for String Orchestra, W19.
Concertino for String Orchestra (arr. piano duet), W110.
Concertino for Two Flutes and Small Orchestra, W35.
Concertino in One Movement for Piano and Orchestra, W29.
Concertino in One Movement for Piano and Orchestra (arr.
    piano duet), W107.
Concertino, No. 2, for Piano and Orchestra, W32.
Concertino, No. 2, for Piano and Orchestra (arr. piano
    duet), W109.
Concerto for Violin and Orchestra, W31.
Concerto for Violin and Orchestra (arr. violin and piano),
    W55.
Country Idylls, Six Pieces for Piano, W75.

Danser la Gigue, W118.
Diversion for Small Orchestra, W22.
Divertimento for Piano and Orchestra, W28.
Divertimento for Piano and Orchestra (arr. piano duet),
    W103.

Etude, W85.
Etude (moto perpetuo), W84.

Fairy Scenes, Suite for Orchestra, W3.
The Fall of the House of Usher, W7.
Fêtes galantes, W136.
Fill a Glass with Golden Wine, W127.
Five Songs, W122.
Five Songs from the "Round Rabbit," W121.
The Flute, Poem for Orchestra, W18.
Four Pieces for Four Hands, W111.
Four Pieces for String Orchestra, W23.
Four Pieces for Wind Instruments, W54.
Four Spanish Songs Transcribed for Piano, W93.
From an Old French Song Book, W135.

The Garden of Shadow, W138.
Granada, W39.

Humoresque, Waltz, Quasi Fox Trot for Clarinet and Piano,
    W50.
Humoresque, Waltz, Quasi Fox Trot for Clarinet and Small
    Orchestra, W26.

Idyl, Elegy, and Scherzo for Flute and Piano, W51.
Impromptu, W90.
In Kensington Gardens, W125.

Jack Frost in Mid-Summer, W36.
Jazz Studies for Two Pianos, W102.

The Land of Love, W144.
Lilacs, W11.
Lilacs (arr. piano duet), W133.
Lullaby for Millicent and Her Mother, W81.
Lyric Piece for Violincello and Orchestra, W34.

March for King James' Entrance (orchestra), W9.
March for King James' Entrance (piano), W79.
Minuet, W77.
The Moth Dance, W99.
Music for English Horn and Orchestra, W33.
Music, When Soft Voices Die, W45.

Nine Waltzes for Orchestra, W8.
Nine Waltzes for Piano, W78.
Nocturne, W112.
Nuns of the Perpetual Adoration, W44.

Ode for Mixed Chorus and Orchestra, W47.
Oh Roses for the Flush of Youth, W145.
Overture for Full Orchestra, W2.

Overture to "She Stoops to Conquer," W1.
The Owl, W131.

Pan and the Star, W37.
Pantomime Sketches for "The Silence of the Harp," W38.
The Parting of Lancelot and Guinevere, W4.
Pastorale for String Quartet, W48.
Pastorale Scarlatti-Tausig, W94.
Peace at Noon, W125.
Piece for Flute, W153.
Piece for Harmonium, W154.
Piece for Violincello and Piano, W70.
Pieces for Organ, W155.
Pierre de Provence to Magnelme the Fair, W120.
Prelude for Orchestra, W24.
Prelude, Toccatina, and Scherzino for Piano, W82.
Prelude to "The Trojan Women," W6.
Preludes to Scenes 1, 2, and 3 of Monaduock Invaded, W114.

Quartet for Piano and Strings, W58.
Quartet for Strings, W57.
Quartet in A minor for Strings, W49.
Quasi Minuetto, W95.
Quasi Polonaise, W83.
Quasi Sarabanda, W96.
Quintet for Clarinet and String Quartet, W62.
Quintet for Piano and Strings, W66.

River Song, W117.
Romance for Baritone and Orchestra, W40.
Romance for Violin and Orchestra, W30.
Romance for Violin and Orchestra (arr. violin and piano),
   W69.

Scentless Gloves I Buy Thee, W128.
Scherzo for Two Pianos and Orchestra, W27.
Seal Lullaby, W146.
Seven Wind Songs, W147.
Sextet for Winds and Piano, W56.
A Siesta, W25.
Silver and Blue, W148.
Sinfonietta for String Orchestra, W16.
Sinfonietta in One Movement for Orchestra, W14.
Sketches after Stephen Crane, W72.
Sonata for Bassoon and Piano, W64.
Sonata for Clarinet (or Violin) and Piano, W53.
Sonata for Flute and Piano, W52.
Sonata for Two Clarinets, op. 43, W59.
Sonata for Two Clarinets, op. 49, W61.
Sonata in F-sharp minor for Pianoforte, W71.
Sonata No. 2 for Piano, W97.
Sonata No. 4 for Piano, W 98.
Sonatina for Cello and Piano, W65.
Sonatina for Clarinet and Piano, W68.
Sonatina for Violin and Piano, W67.
Song for Contralto, W124.
A Song to the Lute, W141.
The Splendor Falls on Castle Walls, W130.

Spring Twilight, W126.
Stevensoniana Suite, W5.
Stevensoniana Suite No. 2, W10.
Study, W73.
Study for Piano, W80.
Suite for String Orchestra, W21.
Sweet and Low, W129.
Symphony in B-flat, W12.
Symphony in B-flat (arr. piano duet), W104.
Symphony No. 2, W13.
Symphony No. 2 (arr. piano duet), W105.
Symphony No. 3, W17.
Symphony No. 3 (arr. piano duet), W108.
Symphony No. 4, W20.
Symphony No. 4 (arr. piano duet), W115.
Synthetic Jazz, W106.

They are not Long the Weeping and the Laughter, W149.
Three Pieces for Flute and Clarinet, W63.
Three Poetical Sketches for Piano, W74.
Three Songs, W137.
Three Songs Without Text, WW142.
Three Songs Without Text With Orchestral Accompaniment, W42.
Toccata, W89.
Toccata giocosa, W91.
Trio for Clarinet, Cello, and Piano, W60.
Two Jazz Studies, W15.
Two Pieces for Piano, Three and Four Hands, W116.

Valser Scherzoso, W87.
Venetian Nights, W133.
Verirrte Reiter, W139.

The Waters are Rising and Flowing, W150.
When Birds are Songless, W151.
When I am Dead my Dearest, W140.
When Lovely Woman Stoops to Folk, W123.

Appendix III:
Chronological Listing
of Original
Compositions

1892

   Pastorale for String Quartet, W48.

1894

   Granada, W39.
   River Song, W117
   Sonata in F-sharp minor for Pianoforte, W71.

1895

   Sketches after Stephen Crane, W72.

1896

   Danser la Gigue, W118.

1897

   All's Well, W119.
   Five Songs from the "Round Rabbit," W121.

1898

   Pierre de Provence to Magnelme the Fair, W120.
   Study, W73.

1899

   Five Songs, W122.
   Three Poetical Sketches for Piano, W74.

1900

    Country Idylls, Six Pieces for Piano, W75.
    When Lovely Woman Stoops to Folk, W123.

1901

    Song for Contralto, W124.

1902

    Lullaby for Millicent and Her Mother, W81.

1903

    At the Grave of a Hero, W76.

1904

    In Kensington Gardens, W125.
    Overture to "She Stoops to Conquer," W1.
    Peace at Noon, W125.
    Spring Twilight, W126.

1905

    Fill a Glass with Golden Wine, W127.

1906
    Nuns of the Perpetual Adoration, W44.
    Scentless Gloves I Buy Thee, W128.

1907

    After Sunset, W134.
    Beside the Idle Summer Sea, W132.
    Fêtes galantes, W136.
    From an Old French Song Book, W135.
    The Owl, W131.
    The Splendor Falls on Castle Walls, W130.
    Sweet and Low, W129.
    Venetian Nights, W133.

1908

    The Garden of Shadow, W138.
    Jack Frost in Mid-Summer, W36.
    The Moth Dance, W99.
    Three Songs, W137.

1910

    Overture for Full Orchestra, W2.
    Verirrte Reiter, W139.
    When I am Dead my Dearest, W140.

1911

  Music, When Soft Voices Die, W45.

1913

  Fairy Scenes, Suite for Orchestra, W3.
  Minuet, W77.
  A Song to the Lute, W141.

1914

  Pan and the Star, W37.

1915

  And the Wilderness Shall Rejoice, W46.
  The Parting of Lancelot and Guinevere, W4.
  Prelude to "The Trojan Women," W6.

1916

  Stevensoniana Suite, W5.

1917

  Pantomime Sketches for "The Silence of the Harp," W38.

1918

  Quartet in A minor for Strings, W49.

1919

  '94 Fox Trot, W100.
  The Fall of the House of Usher, W7.

1920

  Humoresque, Waltz, Quasi Fox Trot for Clarinet and Piano,
    W50.
  Humoresque, Waltz, Quasi Fox Trot for Clarinet and Small
    Orchestra, W 26.
  Nine Waltzes for Orchestra, W8.
  Nine Waltzes for Piano, W78.

1921

  Idyl, Elegy, and Scherzo for Flute and Piano, W51.
  March for King James' Entrance (orchestra), W9.
  March for King James' Entrance (piano), W79.
  Stevensoniana Suite, No. 2, W10.

1922

  Armies in the Fire, W101.

1923

Scherzo for Two Pianos and Orchestra, W27.

1924

Jazz Studies for Two Pianos, W102.

1925

Sonata for Clarinet (or Violin) and Piano, W53.
Sonata for Flute and Piano, W52.

1926

Divertimento for Piano and Orchestra, W28.
Divertimento for Piano and Orchestra (arr. piano duet),
    W103.
Lilacs, W11.

1927

Symphony in B-flat, W12.
Symphony in B-flat (arr. piano duet), W104.

1928

Four Pieces for Wind Instruments, W54.

1929

Symphony No. 2, W13.
Symphony No. 2 (arr. piano duet), W105.
Synthetic Jazz, W106.

1930

Ode for Mixed Chorus and Orchestra, W47.

1931

Concertino in One Movement for Piano and Orchestra, W29.
Concertino in One Movement for Piano and Orchestra (arr.
    piano duet), W107.
Romance for Violin and Orchestra, W30.

1932

Sinfonietta in One Movement for Orchestra, W14.

1933

Concerto for Violin and Orchestra, W31.
Concerto for Violin and Orchestra (arr. violin and piano),
    W55.

1934

Sextet for Winds and Piano, W56.

1935

Two Jazz Studies, W15.
Quartet for Strings, W57.

1936

Sinfonietta for String Orchestra, W16.
Study for Piano, W80.
Symphony No. 3, W17.
Symphony No. 3 (arr. piano duet), W108.

1937

Quartet for Piano and Strings, W58.

1938

Concertino, No. 2, for Piano and Orchestra, W32.
Sonata for Two Clarinets, W61.

1939

Concertino for String Orchestra, W19.
Concertino for String Orchestra (arr. piano duet), W110.
Concertino, No. 2, for Piano and Orchestra (arr. piano
    duet), W109.
The Flute, Poem for Orchestra, W18.
Three Songs Without Text, W142.
Three Songs Without Text With Orchl Accompaniment, W42.

1940

Symphony No. 4, W20.

1941

Trio for Clarinet, Cello, and Piano, W60.

1942

Lullaby for Millicent and Her Mother, W81.
Piece for Flute, W153.
Sonata for Two Clarinets, W61.

1943

Etude, W85.
Etude (moto perpetuo), W84.
Lyric Piece for Violincello and Orchestra, W34.
Music for English Horn and Orchestra, W33.
Prelude, Toccatina, and Scherzino for Piano, W82.
Quasi Polonaise, W83.

1944

   Chimes, W86.
   Quintet for Clarinet and String Quartet, W62.

1945

   Suite for String Orchestra, W21.

1946

   Sonata for Bassoon and Piano, W64.
   Three Pieces for Flute and Clarinet, W63.
   Valser Scherzoso, W87.

1947

   Concertino for Two Flutes and Small Orchestra, W35.
   Diversion for Small Orchestra, W22.
   Four Pieces for Four Hands, W111.
   Four Pieces for String Orchestra, W23.

1948

   Bagatelle for Piano, W88.

1949

   Nocturne, W112.
   Sonatina for Cello and Piano, W65.
   Toccata, W89.

1950

   Quintet for Piano and Strings, W66.

1951

   Sonatina for Violin and Piano, W67.

1952

   Prelude for Orchestra, W24.
   Sonatina for Clarinet and Piano, W68.

1953

   Impromptu, W90.
   Toccata giocosa, W91.

Undated Compositions

   3 Line Piece for Esther Hill, W92.
   Autumn Twilight for Soprano and Orchestra, W41.
   Autumn Twilight for Soprano and Orchestra (arr. voice and
      piano duet), W152.
   The Ballad of Sir Guy, W43.
   By Loe Pool, W143.

Four Spanish Songs Transcribed for Piano, W93.
The Land of Love, W144.
Lilacs (arr. piano duet), W113.
Oh Roses for the flush of youth, W145.
Pastorale Scarlatti-Tausig, W94.
Piece for Harmonium, W154.
Piece for Violincello and Piano, W70.
Pieces for Organ, W155.
Preludes to Scenes 1, 2, and 3 of Monaduock Invaded, W114.
Quasi Minuetto, W95.
Quasi Sarabanda, W96.
Romance for Baritone and Orchestra, W40.
Romance for Violin and Orchestra (arr. violin and piano),
    W69.
Seal Lullaby, W146.
Seven Wind Songs, W147.
A Siesta, W25.
Silver and Blue, W148.
Sonata No. 2 for Piano, W97.
Sonata No. 4 for Piano, W98.
Symphony No. 4 (arr. piano duet), W115.
They are not Long the Weeping and the Laughter, W149.
Two Pieces for Piano, Three and Four Hands, W116.
The Waters are Rising and Flowing, W150.
When Birds are Songless, W151.

Appendix IV:
Listing of Original Compositions by Opus Number

41	Symphony No. 3, W17.
42	Quartet for Piano and Strings, W58.
43	Sonata for Two Clarinets, W59.
44	Concertino, No. 2, for Piano and Orchestra, W32.
45	The Flute, Poem for Orchestra, W18.
46	Concertino for String Orchestra, W19.
47	Symphony No. 4, W20.
48	Trio for Clarinet, Cello, and Piano, W60.
49	Sonata for Two Clarinets, W61.
50	Music for English Horn and Orchestra, W33.
51	Quintet for Clarinet and String Quartet, W62.
51	Lyric Piece for Violincello and Orchestra, W34.

Index

About the Author

LINDA L. TYLER, formerly an instructor of music at the University of California, Santa Cruz, received her Ph.D. from Princeton University and specializes in eighteenth-century music.